WAR DEPARTMENT TECHNICAL MANUAL
TM 11-380

This manual supersedes TM 11-380, 27 April 1942, and TM 11-380B, 20 September 1943

M-209 CONVERTER ENCRYPTION MACHINE TECHNICAL MANUAL
1944 REVISED EDITION

by WAR DEPARTMENT

WAR DEPARTMENT   *17 MARCH 1944*

RESTRICTED. *DISSEMINATION OF RESTRICTED MATTER.* The information contained in restricted documents and the essential characteristics of restricted materiel may be given to any person known to be in the service of the United States and to persons of undoubted loyalty and discretion who are cooperating in Government work, but will not be communicated to the public or to the press except by authorized military public relations agencies. (See also par. 18*b*, AR 380-5, 28 Sep 1942.)

©2012 Periscope Film LLC
All Rights Reserved
ISBN #978-1-937684-69-3

WAR DEPARTMENT TECHNICAL MANUAL
TM 11-380

*This manual supersedes TM 11-380, 27 April
1942, and TM 11-380B, 20 September 1943*

Converter M-209, M-209-A, M-209-B (cipher)

WAR DEPARTMENT   *17 MARCH 1944*

RESTRICTED. *DISSEMINATION OF RESTRICTED MATTER.* The information contained in restricted documents and the essential characteristics of restricted materiel may be given to any person known to be in the service of the United States and to persons of undoubted loyalty and discretion who are cooperating in Government work, but will not be communicated to the public or to the press except by authorized military public relations agencies. (See also par. 18*b*, AR 380-5, 28 Sep 1942.)

WAR DEPARTMENT,
WASHINGTON 25, D. C., 17 MARCH 1944.

TM 11-380, Converter M-209, M-209-A, M-209-B, is published for the information and guidance of all concerned.

(A. G. 300.7 (31 Jan. 44).)

BY ORDER OF THE SECRETARY OF WAR:

G. C. MARSHALL,
Chief of Staff.

OFFICIAL:
J. A. ULIO,
*Major General,
The Adjutant General.*

DISTRIBUTION: IR 5, 7, 17, (2); IBn & H 1 (2); IBn 5, 6, 7, 9, 10, 11, 17 (5); IC 2, 5-11, 17, 18, 44 (3).

(For explanation of symbols see FM 21-6.)

TABLE OF CONTENTS

Section		Par.	Page
I.	Description.		
	General	1	1
	Purpose	2	1
	Main components and accessories	3	2
	Identification of parts	4	2
	Principal operating parts	5	5
II.	Installation and operation.		
	Cryptographic systems	6	9
	Keying elements	7	10
	Preparing for operation	8	11
	Indicators	9	19
	Encipherment	10	21
	Decipherment	11	23
	Zeroizing the machine	12	24
	Spacing	13	24
	Use of letter counter	14	24
	Causes and correction of garbles	15	25
	Operating cautions	16	30
	Security cautions	17	32
III.	Functioning of parts.		
	Theory of operation	18	33
	Key wheel assembly	19	34
	Guide arms	20	35
	Drum assembly	21	35
	Typewheel assembly and print arm assembly	22	37
	Paper feed assembly	23	44

		Par.	Page
IV.	Maintenance.		
	Care of converter	24	45
	Jamming	25	47
	Minor key wheel repairs	26	49
	Minor guide arm repairs	27	50
	Minor drum assembly repairs	28	50
	Minor typewheel assembly repairs	29	51
	Improper printing	30	51
	Improper feeding of paper tape	31	52
	Improper counting	32	53
	Common mechanical failures	33	53
	Procedure for dismantling	34	54
	Procedure for reassembling	35	56
	Inspection check	36	58
V.	Supplementary data.		
	Tabular list of replaceable parts	37	62
Appendix I.	Preparation of pin and lug settings		70
II.	Sets of numbers and overlaps for lug settings		76

LIST OF ILLUSTRATIONS

Fig. No.	Title	Page
1	Main components and accessories	3
2	Converter M-209-(*) open for operation	4
3	Inside view of Converter M-209-(*)	7
4	Converter M-209-(*) strapped to knee	12
5	Setting key wheel pins	14
6	Setting drum bar lugs	16
7	Converter set to make 26-letter check	18
8	Key wheel assembly	38–39
9	Guide arms	36
10	Drum assembly	40
11	Typewheel assembly	42
12	Paper feed assembly	43

DESTRUCTION NOTICE

WHY —To prevent the enemy from using or salvaging this equipment for his benefit.

WHEN—When ordered by your commander.

HOW —1. Smash—Use sledges, axes, handaxes, pickaxes, hammers, crowbars, heavy tools, heel of a boot, etc.

2. Cut—Use axes, handaxes, machetes, etc.

3. Burn—Use gasoline, kerosene, oil, flame throwers, incendiary grenades, etc.

4. Explosives—Use firearms, grenades, TNT, etc.

5. Disposal—Bury in slit trenches, fox holes, other holes. Throw in streams. Scatter.

USE ANYTHING IMMEDIATELY AVAILABLE FOR DESTRUCTION OF THIS EQUIPMENT.

PRELIMINARY—1. *Move all drum bar lugs to zero positions.*

2. *Move all key wheel pins to left positions.*

WHAT—1. Smash—Drum bars, key wheels, guide arms, typewheel, gears, levers.

2. Cut—Canvas case, straps.

3. Burn—Cipher-key lists, technical manuals, paper tape, canvas case.

4. Bury or scatter—Any or all of the above pieces after breaking.

DESTROY EVERYTHING

RESTRICTED

This manual supersedes TM 11-380, 27 April 1942, and TM 11-380B, 20 September 1943.

SECTION I
DESCRIPTION

1. GENERAL.

a. Converter M-209-(*) is a cryptographic device issued by the Signal Corps for use in divisions and lower units, down to and including battalions. It may also be used by units larger than division, or by any other organization authorized by the Chief Signal Officer. The converter provides a secure and rapid method of cryptographing tactical messages, and may be operated by personnel not extensively trained in cryptography.

b. Instructions in this manual are applicable to all cryptographic systems using Converter M-209-(*), as modified by publications used with a particular system. The symbol (*) is used throughout this manual to refer to Converters M-209, M-209-A, and M-209-B.

2. PURPOSE.

a. Converter M-209-(*) is a small, compact, hand-operated tape-printing, mechanical device designed for rapid enciphering and deciphering of tactical messages. When properly set and operated, it will encipher a plain text message of any length, automatically printing the enciphered text on a paper tape in 5-letter groups; or it will decipher a message that has been previously cryptographed by another Converter M-209-(*), printing the clear text on a paper tape with proper spacing between words.

b. The converter is contained in a metal box, and is normally carried in a canvas case, suspended by a strap over the shoulder. The case has compartments for carrying the manual, pencils, extra tape, message books, and message clips. Inside the cover of the converter are clamps for holding a screw driver, a pair of tweezers, an oil can, an ink pad can, and the roll of paper tape in use. When desired, a hand-carrying strap may be attached to the left side of the machine.

3. MAIN COMPONENTS AND ACCESSORIES.

a. Converter M-209-(*) consists of the following main component parts with weights and dimensions as shown (fig. 1):

Quantity	*Part*	*Dimensions (inches)*	*Weight (pounds)*
1	Converter M-209-(*)	7¼ x 5⅞ x 3½	6
1	Case, canvas (complete with straps)	8¼ x 6½ x 6	1
1	Strap, hand-carrying (complete with snaps)	11⅝ long	..

b. The following accessories are issued with the converter:

Quantity	*Part*	*Dimensions (inches)*
1	Can, oil, with cover	2⅝ x ⅜
1	Can, ink pad, with cover	2⅜ x ⅜
1	Screw driver	4 long (2¾ blade, 3/16 tip)
1	Tweezers	4 long
5	Pad, ink (inside ink pad can)	....
2	Tape paper rolls (1 in use, 1 spare)	4 diam. approx.; ⅜ wide
4	Clips, message	....
2	TM 11-380	....

c. The total weight of Converter M-209-(*), including its accessories, is approximately 7¼ pounds. It weighs about 10 pounds when packed for shipment in this country, and has a volume of about 0.37 cubic foot.

4. IDENTIFICATION OF PARTS.

a. Preliminary Procedure. Open the outer cover of the machine by pushing the button located in the center of the front of the cover. Raise the inner lid from the front by lifting it off its spring catch.

DESCRIPTION

TM 11-380
Par. 3-4

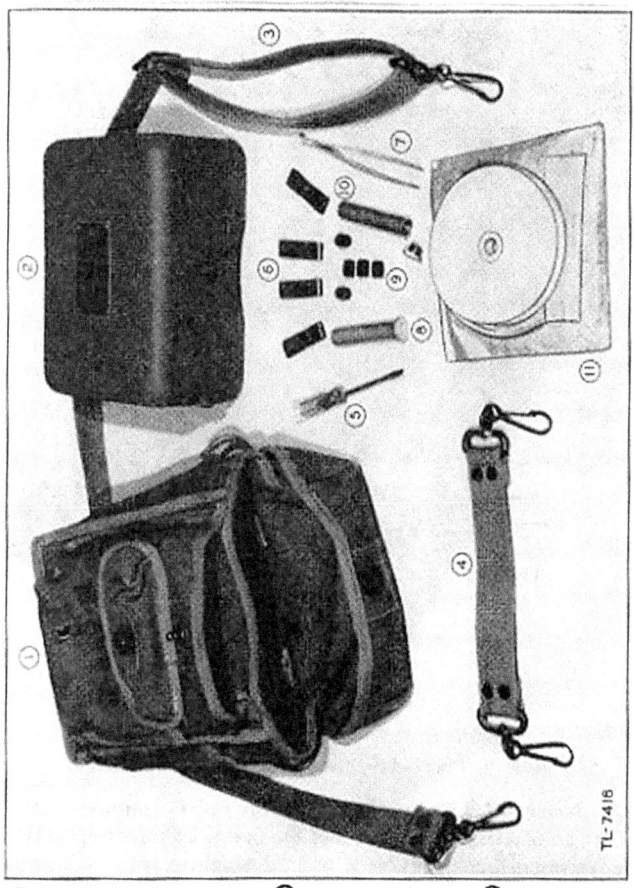

① Canvas case.
② Converter M-209-(*).
③ Carrying strap.
④ Hand strap.
⑤ Screw driver.
⑥ Message clips.
⑦ Tweezers.
⑧ Oil can.
⑨ Ink pads.
⑩ Ink pad can.
⑪ Paper tape.

FIGURE 1. *Main components and accessories.*

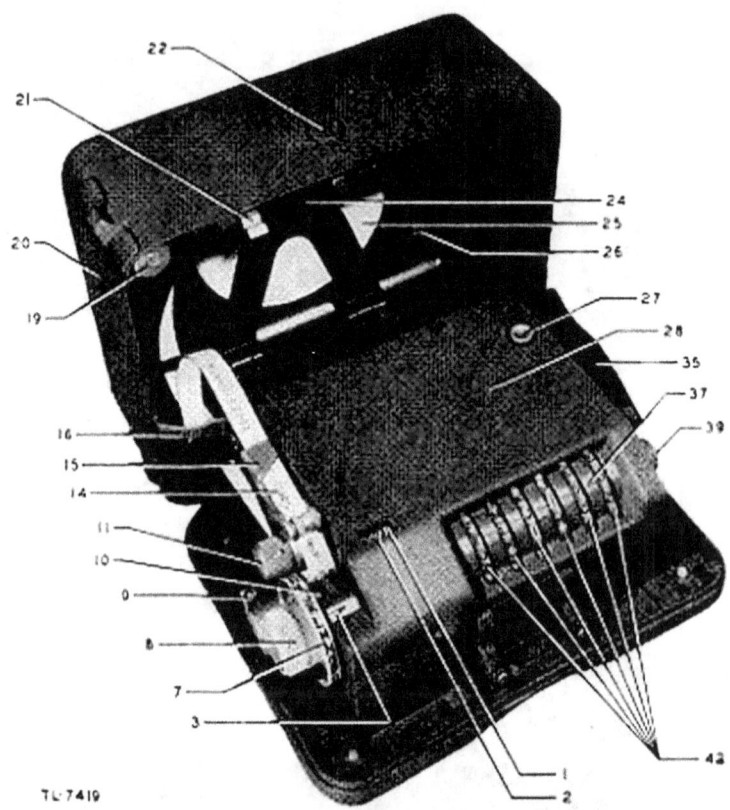

FIGURE 2. *Converter M-209-(*) open for operation.*

b. Numbered Reference List. Operators of Converter M-209-(*) can identify all the parts of the device by referring to the following list and figures 2 and 3. Numbers in parentheses such as (10) correspond to those in figures 2 and 3, and should be studied with an opened converter nearby so that each part may be located. These numbers will be used throughout this manual to assist in identifying parts.

(1) Letter counter window.	(23) Paper guard catch.
(2) Letter counter.	(24) Paper guard.
(3) Indicating index.	(25) Paper roll.
(4) Ink pad.	(26) Tweezers.
(5) Typewheel.	(27) Reset button.
(6) Reproducing disk.	(28) Inner lid.
(7) Indicating disk.	(29) Number plate.
(8) Setting knob.	(30) Drum disks.
(9) Encipher-decipher knob.	(31) Drum bar.
(10) Reading window.	(32) Drum bar lug.
(11) Paper feed knob.	(33) Interlock lever.
(12) Paper feed ratchet.	(34) Guide arm.
(13) 5-letter cam.	(35) Drive knob.
(14) Paper tape.	(36) Intermediate gear.
(15) Paper pressure arm.	(37) Key wheel bench mark.
(16) Cover support.	(38) Key wheel gear.
(17) Ink pad container.	(39) Reset knob.
(18) Screwdriver.	(40) Ineffective pin.
(19) Oil can.	(41) Effective pin.
(20) Outer cover.	(42) Key wheels.
(21) Catch for inner lid.	(43) Typewheel gear.
(22) Cover catch button.	

5. PRINCIPAL OPERATING PARTS.

a. Key Wheels (42). (1) Letters of the alphabet in normal sequence are engraved on the rims of the six key wheels. On each wheel, from left to right, there is a decreasing number of letters. The letters are arranged on the key wheels as follows:

Wheel No.	No. of letters	Letters
1	26	A – Z
2	25	A – Z, omitting W
3	23	A – X, omitting W
4	21	A – U
5	19	A – S
6	17	A – Q

(2) Near the rim of the key wheels, and just below each letter, a small pin projects from one side or the other of the key wheels. The *key wheel pins* may be pushed from side to side in the slots in which they are set. The letters and pins are arranged as part of the preliminary setting of the device and are explained in detail in paragraph 7. The key wheels are mounted on a shaft, on the right end of which is the *reset knob* (39). The key wheels may be turned as a unit in either direction when the *reset button* (27) is depressed and the reset knob twisted. Individual wheels may be turned by hand in one direction only.

b. Indicating Disk (7). The indicating disk is the larger of two disks located on the left-hand side of the converter. Letters of the alphabet are arranged on its rim in normal order. The disk can be rotated freely in either direction, allowing any letter to be aligned on a white bench mark, called the *indicating index* (3). The large knob on the left of the indicating disk is used for turning the disk to the desired letter.

c. Reproducing Disk (6). The letters of the alphabet are engraved in reverse order upon the reproducing disk, the smaller disk located just to the right of and on the same shaft as the indicating disk. When the inner lid is closed, four of the letters can be seen through the *reading window* (10) on the edge of the inner lid. The first letter, nearest the front of the machine, is read when this disk is used (pars. 10*b*(5) and 22*b*).

d. Typewheel (5). The typewheel is mounted on the same shaft with the two disks mentioned above. On its rim are raised letters for printing. These letters are also in reverse order. The last letter printed and the letter which is read on the reproducing disk are the same.

e. Paper Feed Knob (11). The paper tape is advanced automatically when the converter is operated, and also can be fed through the rollers by turning the paper feed knob. The knob turns toward the rear of the machine only.

CONVERTER M-209, M-209-A, M-209-B (CIPHER) TM 11-380

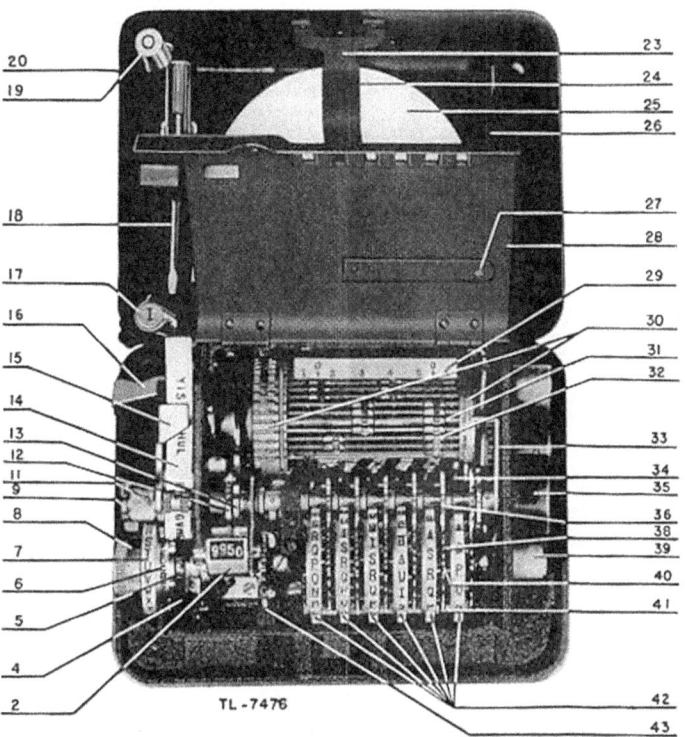

FIGURE 3. *Inside view of Converter M-209-(*).*

f. Paper Pressure Arm (15). On the front end of the paper pressure arm is a small, knurled roller which is held firmly against a larger roller by spring tension. To raise the roller, push down on the rear end of the pressure arm. The roller and arm are used to guide the paper tape. A *cutting edge* is provided on the end of the pressure arm to facilitate tearing off the tape.

g. Letter Counter (2). The letter counter is visible through a window in the left front corner of the converter. It counts letters enciphered or deciphered up to 9999. The counter is returned to zero by turning the *reset knob* (39) in either direction while depressing the *reset button* (27) on top of the inner lid.

h. Encipher-Decipher Knob (9). Just below the paper feed knob is the encipher-decipher knob. When turned to the "C" position, the converter is set for enciphering clear text; when set in "D" position, it is ready to decipher cryptographed text. The position of this knob should be checked before operation.

i. Drive Knob (35). The large black operating handle on the right-hand side of the machine is the drive knob. Each time the indicating disk is moved, the drive knob may be turned once and then locks. At each turn of the drive knob, the machine enciphers or deciphers a letter and prints the equivalent letter on the tape.

j. Drum. When the inner lid is open, the drum can be seen at the rear of the machine. On the drum are 27 *drum bars* (31), which occupy about two-thirds of the circumference of the drum and are numbered at the right of the drum. On each drum bar are two movable lugs which may be set in any one of eight positions, numbered 1 $\overset{0}{\downarrow}$ 2 3 4 5 $\overset{0}{\downarrow}$ 6. Each lug fits into a small hole at each position. It must be pushed slightly toward the front of the machine before it can be disengaged from one hole and slid along the bar into another. When placed at any position, *the lug must always be fitted into the hole provided for it.*

TM 11-380
Par. 6

SECTION II

INSTALLATION AND OPERATION

6. CRYPTOGRAPHIC SYSTEMS.

a. Definition. A military cryptographic system comprises a prearranged set of rules and equipment chosen for cryptographing messages sent from one unit to another. All systems fall into one of two classifications, *code* or *cipher*. In code systems, groups of letters or numbers represent words, phrases, or entire sentences. A cipher system normally uses single letters to represent other single letters. Converter M-209-(*) is a cipher device since, when operated, it substitutes a letter for a letter.

b. Cipher Keys. Every cipher system must be provided with a guide, or *cipher key*, for its operation. The cipher key should be changed as often as is necessary to preserve the security of the system. The key for systems using Converter M-209-(*) must include two tables which make up a *cipher-key* list and are published periodically in a system publication or the signal operation instructions of a using unit. The tables, changed only by order of the signal or communication officer, govern preliminary settings which must be made before enciphering or deciphering a message. The proper use of cipher-key lists is explained in paragraph 8.

c. Converter M-209-(*) Systems. Any cipher system employing the Converter M-209-(*) must consist of the following:

(1) The Converter M-209-(*).

(2) This manual which contains operating instructions for the Converter M-209-(*).

(3) The cipher-key list which is in effect at the time.

(4) A system publication describing the particular system in use at the time, or personal instruction in such a system.

7. KEYING ELEMENTS. Units using Converter M-209-(*) must make certain that the following keying elements are set identically if they are to exchange messages:

a. External Keying Element. The external keying element is composed of the six key wheels (42). Letters on the key wheels are selected at random by the enciphering operator, and lined up from left to right along the white bench mark. *Different letters must be selected for every message.* These six letters make up the message indicator and are transmitted with the message (par. 9).

b. Internal Keying Elements. There are two internal keying elements; each is initially set, and changed, in accordance with a cipher-key list. The first internal keying element is made up of the key wheel pins (40), (41). When placed to the right, or effective, position, the pins affect the operation of the machine; to the left, they are in a *noneffective* position. The second internal keying element is made up of the movable lugs (32) on the drum bars (31). Lugs are effective in any position except the two marked " $\overset{0}{\downarrow}$." Instructions for setting the keying elements are in paragraph 8.

c. Changes of Keys. A high degree of cryptographic security is provided when Converter M-209-(*) is used. Systems using Converter M-209-(*), however, can be solved, especially if a large volume of traffic is enciphered without changing the arrangement of the keying elements. A *daily* change in the internal keying elements is advisable, although the frequency of change will depend upon the tactical situation. This is the responsibility of the signal or communication officer. *Changes in the external keying element are the responsibility of the*

INSTALLATION AND OPERATION
TM 11-380
Par. 7-8

operator alone, and must be made for every message he enciphers. There is no reason for allowing the enemy to "break" a message enciphered with Converter M-209-(*) because the keying elements were not changed often enough. The key wheel alignments should be noted to prevent using the same arrangement of letters for future messages.

8. PREPARING FOR OPERATION.

a. General. The procedure given in this paragraph is intended to show the operator how to install the converter and make all preliminary settings.

b. Installation. Normally Converter M-209-(*) will be operated under cover to protect the machine from dust and dampness. Usually the converter will be set up on a table or some solid support. If necessary, the machine may be secured to the operator's knee in the following manner: Attach the carrying strap to the bottom of the converter and pass it under the operator's foot. Shorten or lengthen the strap so that the converter will be held firmly in place on the knee. The base of the machine is shaped to fit the curvature of the knee (fig. 4).

c. Key Wheel Pins. Open the outer cover of the converter, and raise the inner lid. If the machine has been properly zeroized (par. 12), all of the key wheel pins will project from the left-hand side of the key wheels. If any project from the right-hand side, use the screw driver provided and push them to the left. This will make the setting easier. Set the pins as indicated in table I, *Position of key wheel pins.* The columns of letters and dashes represent the six key wheels, from left to right. The pins associated with the letters which are printed in the columns are to be pushed to the right, or effective, position. Where a dash appears, the pin associated with the omitted letter will remain at the left, or ineffective, position. Thus, following the example table, the pin under

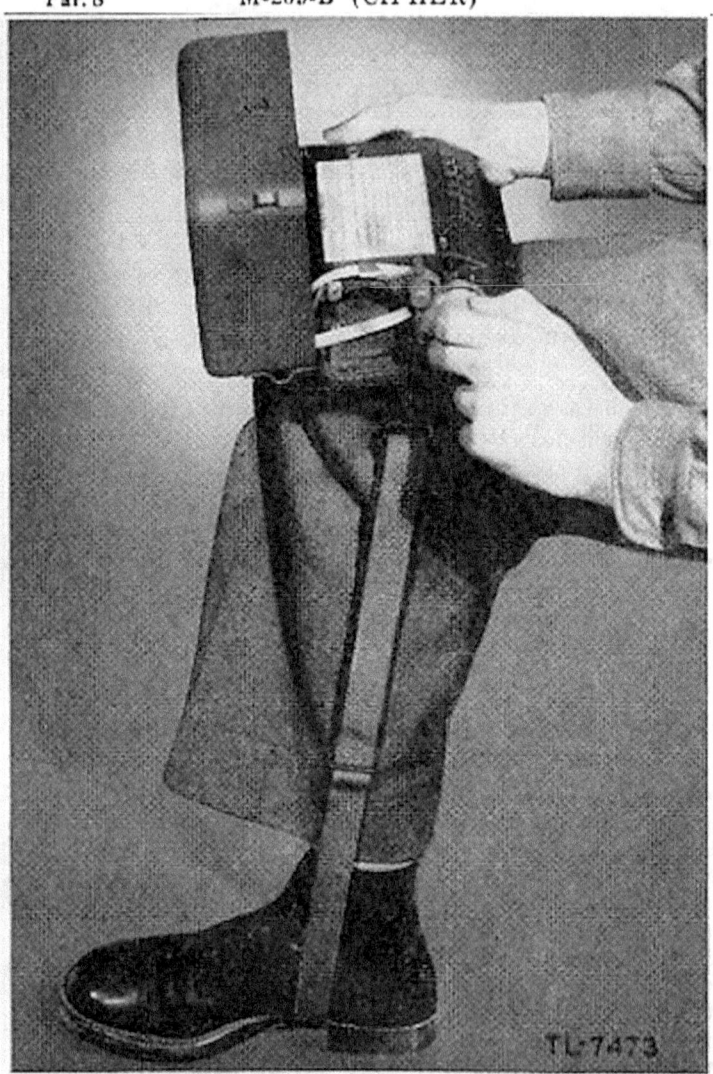

FIGURE 4. *Converter M-209-(*) strapped to knee.*

INSTALLATION AND OPERATION TM 11-380 Par. 8

letter A on wheel number 1 should be moved to the right or effective position. The pin under letter C on wheel number 1 will remain at the left, or ineffective, position. A knife blade or the special screw driver provided may be used to set the pins (fig. 5). Each pin must be moved all the way to the left

TABLE I. *Position of key wheel pins.*

Period (date) to (date).

No. 1 (26)	No. 2 (25)	No. 3 (23)	No. 4 (21)	No. 5 (19)	No. 6 (17)
A	A	A	—	—	A
B	—	B	—	B	B
—	—	—	C	—	—
D	D	—	—	D	D
—	E	—	E	E	—
—	—	—	F	F	—
—	G	G	—	—	—
H	—	H	H	H	H
I	—	—	I	I	—
—	J	J	—	—	—
K	K	—	—	—	K
—	L	L	—	—	—
M	—	M	M	M	—
N	—	N	N	N	N
—	O	—	—	—	O
—	—	—	P	P	—
—	—	—	—	—	Q
—	R	R	—	—	
S	S	S	S	S	
T	—	T	T		
—	U	U	U		
V	—	—			
W	X	X			
—	—				
—	—				
—					

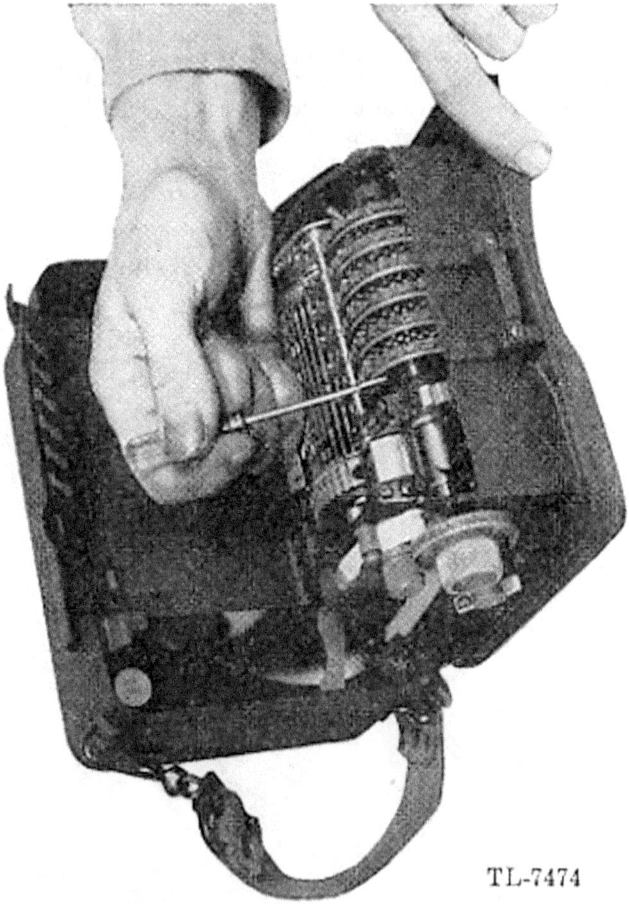

TM 11-380 CONVERTER M-209, M-209-A,
Par. 8   M-209-B (CIPHER)

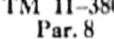

FIGURE 5. *Setting key wheel pins.*

INSTALLATION AND	TM 11-380
OPERATION	Par. 8

or right. A garble will result if pins are left in an intermediate position. Care in making the setting will prevent loss of time later. The effective period for that particular setting must be known in order that a new setting will be made at the proper time. (Information regarding the preparation of a table of pin settings will be found in appendix I.)

TABLE II. *Position of drum bar lugs.*

Period (date) to (date).

1.	3–6	10.	2–0	19.	2–0
2.	0–6	11.	2–0	20.	2–5
3.	1–6	12.	2–0	21.	2–5
4.	1–5	13.	2–0	22.	0–5
5.	4–5	14.	2–0	23.	0–5
6.	0–4	15.	2–0	24.	0–5
7.	0–4	16.	2–0	25.	0–5
8.	0–4	17.	2–0	26.	0–5
9.	0–4	18.	2–0	27.	0–5

26-letter check

T N J U W A U Q T K C Z K N U T O T B C W A R M I O

d. Drum Bar Lugs. With the inner lid open, the drum will be seen in the rear of the machine. Each of the 27 drum bars has 2 movable lugs which may be placed in effective positions 1 through 6, or in 2 noneffective positions labeled "0." Consult table II, *Position of drum bar lugs.* The 2 columns of numbers, 1 through 14, and 15 through 27, represent the 27 drum bars. The numbers opposite each drum bar number denote the positions which the two lugs on each drum bar will occupy. These positions are indicated on the machine by the number plate behind the drum. For example, on bar 1, the left-hand lug will be moved to position 3 and the right-hand lug to position 6. On bar 2, the left-hand lug will be moved to the

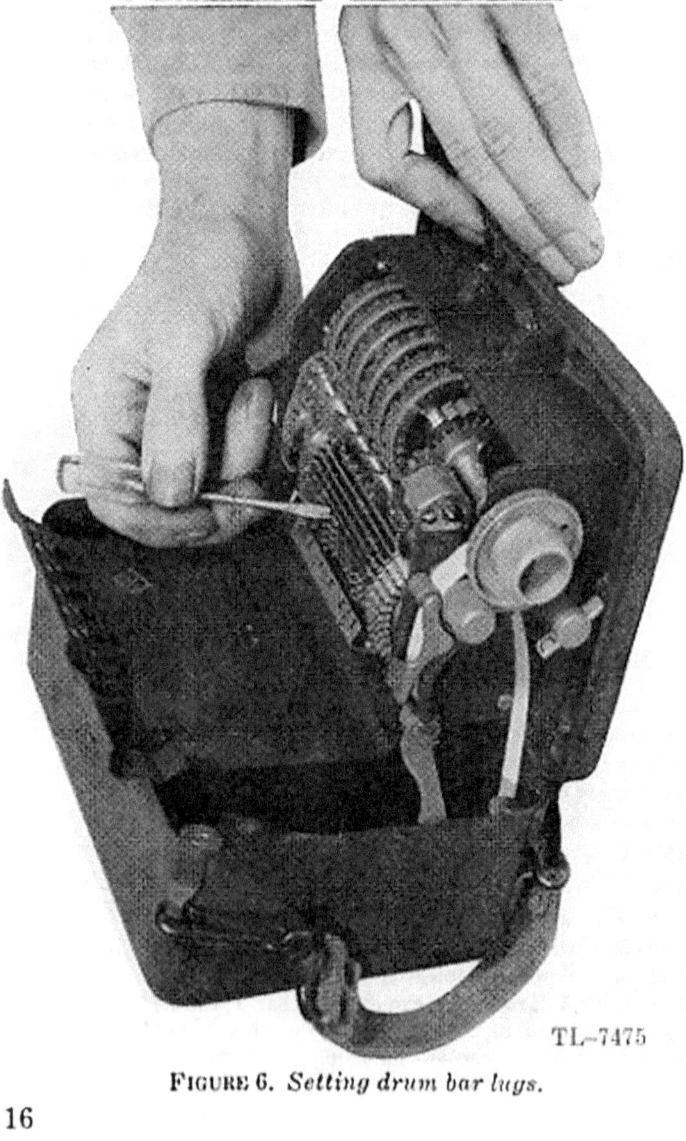

TM 11–380 CONVERTER M-209, M-209-A,
Par. 8   M-209-B (CIPHER)

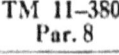

FIGURE 6. *Setting drum bar lugs.*

left zero position, and the right-hand lug to position 6. Turn the setting knob (8) to release the drum lock and to allow the drive knob to rotate the drum. Use the special screwdriver provided to move the lugs from one position to another (fig. 6). When correctly placed, each lug will lock in position in a small hole. When moving a lug, push it slightly toward the front of the machine to release it, before attempting to slide it to another location. *Be sure that the lug catches in the hole at the new position.* If a lug is allowed to remain in an intermediate position, it will jam the machine. A click can be heard when the lug is properly placed. It is recommended that the left-hand lugs on each drum bar be placed in positions 1, 2, 3, and the left zero, and that the right-hand lugs be placed in positions 4, 5, 6, and the right zero. When all lugs have been properly set, turn the drive knob until the drum locks into place. (Information on the preparation of a table of lug settings may be found in appendix I.)

e. Twenty-six-letter Check. Every cipher-key list will include a 26-letter check. Using this check, the operator of Converter M-209-(*) may verify his preliminary settings. The operator must always make the check immediately after completing his pin and lug settings. The following steps are necessary: Insert the paper tape according to instructions given in paragraph 24*d*. Make certain that the ink pad contains enough ink for legible printing. (If it does not, replace the pad from the ink pad can clamped to the outer cover.) Turn the setting knob several times to ink the typewheel thoroughly. With the inner lid closed, depress the reset button and turn the reset knob to zeroize the letter counter. The right-hand zero of the letter counter must be completely in view. A click will be heard when it comes into place. Set the encipher-decipher knob in the C position. Set the initial alignment of AAAAAA on the key wheels by turning them individually until the letter A of each wheel lines up with the white bench mark (fig. 7). Turn the indicating disk until the letter A is on line

① Counter set on 0000.
② Encipher-decipher knob set in the C position.
③ Key wheels aligned to AAAAAA.
④ First letter A located on indicating disk.

FIGURE 7. *Converter set to make 26-letter check.*

INSTALLATION AND TM 11-380
OPERATION Par. 8-9

with the indicating index, and encipher it by operating the drive knob. Be sure that the drive knob is turned until it locks in place. Continue the encipherment of "A's" in the same manner until the letter counter shows that 26 letters have been enciphered. If the letter A is already aligned on the indicating index at the end of an operating cycle, the indicating disk must be moved to another letter and returned to A in order to release the drum lock, which prevents turning the drive knob. Advance the paper tape by turning the paper feed knob until the paper can be torn off at the cutting edge. Compare the tape with the 26-letter check in the cipher-key list. If the tape and the 26-letter check are identical, the pin and lug settings are correct; if they differ by one or more letters, there is an error in the initial settings of the converter which must be corrected before proceeding with any encipherment or decipherment. Refer to the cipher-key list composed of tables 1 and 2, and make the preliminary settings. Verify these settings by means of the 26-letter check in table II.

9. INDICATORS.

a. General. Every message enciphered with Converter M-209-(*) will be accompanied by certain *indicators* which are transmitted with the message. The purpose of these indicators is to show the deciphering operator what settings to make on his machine before deciphering that message. The various methods of determining and using the indicators are described in system publications.

b. Types. Three types of *indicators* are used. The number required will depend upon the system.

(1) The *system indicator* discloses to the receiving operator the system which is in use. It will appear in the system publication or the signal operation instructions.

(2) The message indicator reveals to the deciphering operator the initial key wheel alignment which was used to encipher

19

the message (par. 7a). In some systems this indicator will be enciphered before transmission to provide additional security.

(3) The *cipher-key indicator* designates the particular cipher-key list which was in effect at the time of encipherment. This indicator will appear in the SOI with the cipher-key lists.

  c. Use. The following method of using the indicators is intended as an example for training purposes only:

(1) The system indicator is composed of two letters, such as FW. This system indicator designates the method of cryptographing, and is placed as the first two letters of the first group of the indicators.

(2) The message indicator is taken from the six key wheels before encipherment is begun, by reading the letters which are aligned with the white bench mark. These six letters are divided in half, the first half forms the last three letters of the first indicator group, and the second half forms the first three letters of the second indicator group. These appear as the first two groups of a message, and are sent in the clear. Assume, for example, that the initial key wheel alignment is QAHNKE. These letters make up the message indicator, and are written in the form shown below.

(3) The cipher-key indicator will appear as two letters, such as LP, accompanying each cipher-key list. These letters are inserted as the last two of the second indicator group.

(4) The two indicator groups would be made up and transmitted as follows:

FW QAH   NKE LP
‾‾ ‾‾‾   ‾‾‾ ‾‾
(1) (2)   (3)

This is only a sample method of showing the indicators.

  d. The indicators will always be placed in the order shown above, and will be inserted before the first group of cipher

INSTALLATION AND TM 11-380
OPERATION Par. 9-10

text. They also appear (in the same order) as the last two groups of the message, following the last group of cipher text. The indicators must be added in pencil in both cases.

10. ENCIPHERMENT.

a. General. The student should follow the procedure on a converter which has been set and checked with the cipher-key list composed of tables I and II.

b. Preliminary Instructions. The following steps for enciphering a message with Converter M-209-(*) are presented in a numbered sequence designed to help an operator learn the process by performing the operations:

(1) Make certain that the drive knob is in the locked position. If it is not locked, turn it until it clicks and will turn no more. The knob cannot be turned again until the indicating disk has been moved. Leave the drive knob in the locked position until all adjustments have been made.

(2) Turn the encipher-decipher knob so that the letter C is up and facing the front.

(3) Zeroize the letter counter. This will insure that the enciphered text will be printed in groups of five letters, and will show the exact number of letters enciphered.

(4) Align the key wheels at random. In selecting the key wheel alignment, the operator should move the key wheels individually, choosing the letters which line up on the white bench mark. These letters should not spell a word, nor should the same letter be found twice in one key wheel alignment. The flat end of the tweezers may be used for turning the key wheels individually. *Do not use an eraser tip.* Each key wheel upon coming into place will click audibly; do not leave a key wheel in an intermediate position. Make a note of the indicator so that it may be referred to later.

(5) Advance enough paper tape to allow insertion of the system and message indicators by hand. (If the supply of paper tape is exhausted, the cipher text may be copied from the reproducing disk, as each letter is enciphered.)

c. Procedure. Encipher the following message: REINFORCEMENTS URGENTLY NEEDED. Proceed as follows:

(1) Turn the indicating disk until the first letter to be enciphered (R) lines up with the indicating index, and release the knob.

(2) Turn the drive knob until it locks. Avoid a rapid or jerky movement of the drive knob. A moderate steady motion is preferable. Complete the operating cycle before enciphering another letter, or jamming of the mechanism will result.

(3) Locate the second letter of the message (E) on the indicating disk and rotate the drive knob again. This procedure is repeated for all letters of the clear text.

(4) Encipher the letter Z between the words of the clear text; i. e., between *reinforcements* and *urgently*, and between *urgently* and *needed*, in the above message. When the cipher text is deciphered, a space will appear at the proper place between the words. A thorough explanation of Z-spacing is included in paragraph 13*b*.

(5) Since the drive knob is locked at the end of each operating cycle, the indicating disk must always be moved before another letter can be enciphered or deciphered. Occasionally the desired letter is already in position before the indicating disk is moved. If this happens, move the disk to another letter and return it to the desired letter. This will release the lock and allow the drive knob to be turned.

(6) When the message has been completely enciphered, advance the paper tape two or three inches and tear it off at the cutting edge.

INSTALLATION AND　　TM 11-380
OPERATION　　Par. 10-11

(7) Note that the cipher text has been automatically spaced into five letter groups. If the last group contains only 1, 2, 3, or 4 letters, add enough X's in pencil to make it a complete 5-letter group. DO NOT ENCIPHER THESE X's TO COMPLETE THE LAST GROUP. Such a practice reduces the security of the system and aids the enemy in solving the message.

(8) Now print at the beginning of the message the system, message, and cipher key indicators, and repeat them in that order at the end of the message. From this point, the code clerk will follow the procedure for cryptographed messages as outlined in FM 24-5, Basic Signal Communication, or the standing operating procedure of his unit.

11. DECIPHERMENT. The deciphering operator must have initial settings on his machine which are identical to those used by the enciphering operator. Retaining the settings of tables I and II, decipher the message which was enciphered in paragraph 10c. Proceed as follows:

a. Make certain that the drive knob is in a locked position.

b. Turn the encipher-decipher knob to the D position.

c. Zeroize the letter counter.

d. Check the message indicators at the beginning of the message with those at the end to make sure that they are the same, and align the key wheels in accordance with the message indicator.

e. Proceed as in encipherment; locate the cipher letters one by one on the indicating disk, and operate the drive knob in one complete cycle each time. Disregard the spaces between the groups of the cipher text. Carry in mind one 5-letter group at a time so that it will not be necessary to look at the text for each letter; this will keep errors at a minimum.

f. Upon completion of decipherment, advance the tape until the printed clear text is beyond the cutting edge, and tear it off. If the letter "Z" was used as a space between words when the message was enciphered, the clear text will appear in its original word form. Local message center procedure will be followed in servicing the message and delivering it to the addressee.

12. ZEROIZING THE MACHINE. When the converter is to be closed at the end of a day or a period of operation, the internal keying elements of the device must be zeroized. First, push all of the key wheel pins to the left or ineffective position. Second, move all lugs to the zero positions on the drum bars. Tear off any tape which contains printing, and close the outer cover of the machine. The converter should then be placed in the canvas case provided, and kept in a dry place until used again.

13. SPACING.

a. Automatic Spacing. Five-letter cipher groups are obtained only when the encipher-decipher knob is set in the encipher position. This spacing is automatic and is ignored by both enciphering and deciphering operators.

b. Z-spacing. If the operator enciphers a Z for each space between words of clear text, the deciphered message will appear in its original word form (par. 10c(4)). This is made possible by the elimination of the letter Z in the deciphering process. Such a word as ORGANIZED will appear in clear text as ORGANI ED, but the missing letter can easily be supplied from the context of the message. The printing of the Z is prevented only when the encipher-decipher knob is set for deciphering.

14. USE OF LETTER COUNTER. An operator who wishes to check a word or correct an error, or who has lost his place in the message he is enciphering or deciphering, need not

INSTALLATION AND OPERATION

start at the beginning of the message if he has a proper understanding of the letter counter. Whenever it is necessary to check back in the message for any reason, proceed as follows:

a. Determine the place in the message where the error occurs. Count the letters from the beginning of the message to the error. If the count is made from clear text, remember to count spaces also. In cipher text, the number of groups can be multiplied by five (there are five letters in each group), and any extra letters which are correct can be added to the product. For example, in the message used in paragraph 10c, "REINFORCEMENTS URGENTLY NEEDED," a mistake might have been caused by skipping a letter in decipherment so that the following text resulted: "REINFORCEMENTS URGENQCTLV etc." A count of the letter in error will show that all letters through the 20th are correct.

b. Turn the letter counter back until it reads 20. Count the cipher text letters up through the 20th (four groups), and begin from there by deciphering the 21st letter. This process may be used for reenciphering or redeciphering any portion of a message as long as the indicators remain the same.

15. CAUSES AND CORRECTION OF GARBLES.

a. General. Faulty operation of a cryptographic device, errors made in transmission, or mistakes made by either the enciphering or deciphering operator may produce garbled text. The garble may be so slight that the text may still be read, or it may likewise be so serious that the text will be unreadable. It is important that operators of Converter M-209-(*) recognize the types of garbles and know their causes, and whenever possible, make correction. *The operator should always make every possible attempt to decipher a message before asking for a service on it.* There are five common causes of garbled text.

b. Incorrectly Set Key Wheel Pin. One incorrectly placed key wheel pin will result in garbled text. This type of garble is recognized by a single-letter error appearing periodically in the text, i. e., by errors which are an equal distance apart. Location of the incorrectly set pin is accomplished in the following manner:

(1) Count the number of letters including spaces from one garbled letter to the next. This number determines the key wheel on which the pin is located. If the count is 17, the incorrectly set pin will be found on wheel number 6 (numbering from left to right), because this wheel contains only 17 pins (table I). If the count is 19, the incorrectly set pin will be found on wheel number 5; if 21, on wheel number 4; if 23, on wheel number 3; if 25, on wheel number 2; if 26, on wheel number 1. The following message is slightly garbled as the result of an incorrectly set key wheel pin:

NOW IS L̲HE TIME FOR ALL X̲OOD MEN

If the deciphering were continued, the error would appear periodically at the same interval. A count shows that from the first error to the second, there are 17 letters and spaces, indicating that the incorrectly-set pin is on key wheel number 6.

(2) Following the directions given in paragraph 14, turn the letter counter to the number of the last letter deciphered before the garbled letter appeared. In the example above, the counter would be turned back to 7.

(3) By using the following table and counting over the top of the key wheel which contains the error, beginning with the letter which is on line with the bench mark, the pin which was in the operation at the time of the error will be located.

Wheel No.	1	2	3	4	5	6
Count back	16	15	14	13	12	11

INSTALLATION AND TM 11-380
OPERATION Par. 15

If A were aligned on the key wheels, the pin in operation for the next letter would be the one associated with the letter P for wheel number 1, O for wheel number 2, N for wheel number 3, and so forth. After determining the pin in error, turn the wheel until that pin is visible, and move it to the other side. Reset the key wheel to its proper place and decipher the letter to determine whether the trouble has been corrected.

c. Incorrectly Set Drum Bar Lug. Garbles caused by an incorrectly set drum bar lug are recognized by a *nonperiodic* appearance of errors throughout the text, which may or may not be readable at first sight. Such garbles can be divided into three types according to the results produced:

(1) The first type is caused by a lug which has been made effective, when it should be noneffective. This condition adds one positive "kick" in the operation of the machine. In this case the letters which are in error will always be those letters which immediately follow the correct letters in the alphabet. The text might appear as follows:

NOX IS THEAUIMF FORAAML HOOE MEN

(NOW IS THE TIME FOR ALL GOOD MEN)

Note that each incorrect letter takes the place of that letter in the alphabet which just precedes it: X for W, A for Z (space), U for T, F for E, and so forth.

(2) The second type is caused by a lug which has been placed in a noneffective position, when it should be in an effective position. This condition results in one less "kick" in the machine's operation; that is, the letter in error will be that letter which immediately precedes the correct letter in the alphabet. The text might appear as follows:

NOV IS THD TIME FOR _KL GOODYMEN

(NOW IS THE TIME FOR ALL GOOD MEN)

Here it can be seen that the incorrect letter V precedes the correct letter W in the alphabet, that D precedes E, and so forth.

(3) A third type of error results when a lug is made effective in the wrong position. For this case there will be both plus and minus "kicks" in the operation of the machine. The result will be that some of the letters in error will be those letters which come immediately before the correct letters in the alphabet, others will be those which come immediately after the correct letters. The garbled text usually has no resemblance to the original clear text, and may appear as follows:

NNWAJTYSHDATHMF FNR LKYGPPD MDN

(NOW IS THE TIME FOR ALL GOOD MEN)

Comparison of the clear text with the garbled text will show that the garbled letters are either immediately before or immediately after the correct letters in the alphabet.

> NOTE: There is no way of finding the particular lug which is in error in the above cases. However, it is possible to obtain clear text if the operator substitutes letters as directed in the preceding paragraphs.

d. Incorrect Setting of Indicator. This mistake will result if the enciphering operator fails to copy down the correct message indicator or cipher key indicator; if the receiving operator records the message improperly; or if the deciphering operator makes an accurate setting. In any case, unreadable text will be the result. Correction can be made only by referring to the correct indicators. Receiving operators must always check the indicators at the end of the message, as well as those at the beginning. These two indicators should be identical, but if they differ, the receiving operator will have to try them both in attempting to decipher the message.

INSTALLATION AND OPERATION

e. Transmission Errors. The frequency of garbles due to transmission errors will depend upon the efficiency of transmitting and receiving operators and upon the quality of transmission. A knowledge of Morse code will help the deciphering operator to see the errors possible due to transmission, and to correct them.

f. Omissions or Repetitions. The deciphering operator's machine may produce readable text up to a point after which a garble appears. The cause of the garble will either be the omission of letters or groups, or the repetition of letters or groups. To determine the cause of the garble, the operator must make several checks.

(1) First, the cryptographed text is examined for the repetition of letters or groups. Identical groups will probably not appear side by side, but may appear as in the following example:

QHKLV NCRQH KLVOP

In this case the operator would turn the counter back to the number just preceding the number of the first repeated letter, and proceed with the decipherment omitting the repeated

(2) If no groups are repeated in the message, each group should be examined to determine whether any group contains more or less than five letters. If a group contains less than five letters, a letter, or letters, has been left out in transmission and the letter counter must be turned up the necessary number of times before proceeding. If a group contains more than five letters, a letter has been added and must be omitted when deciphering.

(3) Trouble may result due to the deciphering operator's carelessness or to an interruption in his work; in which case the letter counter must be turned back to the last letter of clear text (par. 14), before deciphering is continued.

(4) Omission of a code group within a message, during transmission or reception, is one of the most difficult errors to

locate. If an error occurs which is not of a type described in the preceding paragraphs, the operator can assume the omission of one or more groups. The letter counter should be moved up five points from the number of the last correct group before proceeding. If clear text is not obtained by moving the letter counter up 5 points, it should be moved up 10 points, or 15, until clear text is produced.

16. OPERATION CAUTIONS.

a. General. Most failures of Converter M-209-(*) can be credited to careless or faulty operation rather than to the machine. The converter is designed to withstand hard usage in the field, and is therefore rugged in its construction, but it must be handled with a reasonable amount of care if it is to give satisfactory service.

b. Check List. Certain cautions have been mentioned throughout this section of the manual which, if properly observed, will help to keep the machine running smoothly. These cautions appear below as a check list for the new operator:

(1) In making preliminary settings, each key-wheel pin must be pushed all the way to the right or left; do not leave a pin in an intermediate position.

(2) Drum bar lugs must be properly seated in the holes provided for them.

(3) The reset knob must click into place after being turned, and a complete figure must be visible on the letter counter.

(4) Key wheels will click when moved into position. Do not allow a key wheel to remain in an intermediate position.

(5) Turn the drive knob in a complete cycle until it locks. Avoid an excessively rapid or jerky motion.

(6) The indicating disk must not be moved until the drive knob has made a complete cycle.

INSTALLATION AND OPERATION

Table 3. *Garble correction chart.*

Error	Cause	Correction
1. Periodic single-letter error.	Incorrectly set key wheel pin.	Count interval between errors; turn counter back to number before error; count around wheel to pin in effect, change this pin to proper position.
2. Nonperiodic errors (may or may not appear unreadable).	Incorrectly set drum bar lug.	Substitute letters which appear before and after garbled letters in alphabet, and attempt to read the message.
3. Unreadable text.	Incorrect indicator setting.	Obtain correct indicator setting.
4. Nonperiodic errors.	Poor transmission.	Determine meaning from context, or ask for service on message.
5. Clear text up to certain point, followed by garble.	(a) Repetition of letter. (b) Repetition of group. (c) Omission of letter. (d) Omission of group.	(a) Leave out repeated letter. (b) Omit repeated group. (c) Turn letter counter up one. (d) Turn letter counter up five points.

(7) NEVER USE FORCE TO CLEAR A JAMMED MACHINE. Paragraph 25 gives instructions for eliminating a jam.

17. SECURITY CAUTIONS.

a. Change the message indicator for each message sent.

b. Destroy all printed tape not pasted to a message blank.

c. Do not encipher X's to fill out the last cipher group of a message. Complete a group by adding X's in pencil.

d. Be very careful to avoid errors while enciphering. Errors may help an enemy to break down the cryptographic system in use.

TM 11-380
Par. 18

SECTION III

FUNCTIONING OF PARTS

18. THEORY OF OPERATION.

Converter M-209-(*) operates on the cryptographic principal of reciprocal-substitution alphabets. The effect is that of sliding a normal-alphabet sequence against reversed normal alphabet. The manner in which the various elements of the converter shift the alphabets, with respect to each other, produces a high degree of irregularity in the letter substitutions during encipherment. For example, in the enciphering of a message, the alphabets might be arranged in the following manner for the first letter:

A B C D E F G H I J K L M N O P Q R S T U V W X Y Z

K J I H G F E D C B A Z Y X W V U T S R Q P O N M L

Thus, if K were the first letter to be enciphered, its cipher equivalent would be the letter A. For the second letter to be enciphered the alphabets might be arranged as follows:

A B C D E F G H I J K L M N O P Q R S T U V W X Y Z

R Q P O N M L K J I H G F E D C B A Z Y X W V U T S

If K were also the second letter to be enciphered, its cipher equivalent would be the letter H. The continual shifting of the alphabets is the factor which provides security for messages enciphered with Converter M-209-(*).

19. KEY WHEEL ASSEMBLY.

a. The key wheel assembly comprises the six key wheels (42) with their ratchets, pawls, and gears (38); the reset knob (39) and key wheel shaft; the key wheel intermediate gear shaft and gears (36); and the letter counter (2). The key wheel ratchet and pawl arrangement cannot be seen clearly unless the key wheels are removed from the shaft. Figure 8 below shows an inside view of each key wheel gear.

b. The key wheels are operated by the drive knob (35) on the right-hand side of the machine. The key wheel gears are driven by a set of intermediate gears located behind the six key wheels. A key wheel feed-cam assembly on the right drum disk moves the set of intermediate gears one notch each time the drive knob is rotated. The intermediate gears vary in circumference and number of teeth. The smallest gear has the greatest number of teeth, and is located on the left. The largest gear has the smallest number of teeth, and is located on the right. This variation is necessary due to a like variation in the key wheels driven by the intermediate gears. Letters of the alphabet appear in normal order on the outer rim of each key wheel. The key wheel on the left has the greatest number of letters, and the key wheel on the right has the smallest number of letters (par. 5*a*). For each letter on the key wheels there is one pin, and for each pin there is a tooth in the associated key wheel gear. To allow the key wheels to move simultaneously for one space during each operating cycle, the key wheel gears are so constructed that they compensate for the differences in the spacing of the key wheel pins.

c. A ratchet pawl permits turning the key wheels individually by hand, but in one direction only. When the relative positions of the key wheels are changed, different combinations of pins result without resetting all key wheel pins. The letter counter records numbers from 0000 to 9999, and is

FUNCTIONING OF PARTS

driven by a gear on the left-hand side of the intermediate gear shaft. The counter will operate only when the key wheels are turned as a unit. The reset knob will zeroize the letter counter or turn the key wheels back to any previous setting.

d. A different pin on each wheel comes into play for each letter cryptographed, until the wheels have made one complete rotation. However, each key wheel pin is not necessarily in an effective position. Paragraph 8 explains that only those pins which are pushed to the right are effective.

20. GUIDE ARMS. Six guide arms, one for each key wheel, are located between the key wheel assembly and the drum (fig. 9). The guide arms form the link between the key wheels and drum bars. When a key wheel pin in the effective position comes into play the associated guide arm is released allowing the guide arm spring to push the guide arm toward the rear of the machine. In this position, the guide arm will, when the drum is rotated, make contact with the drum bar lugs in line with it. For example, the guide arm for wheel number 6 will contact those lugs which are in the number 6 position on the drum bars. When the drum is turned, the guide arm forces the drum bars it controls to the left, which is their effective position. A key wheel pin in the noneffective position holds the guide arm it controls in an inactive position. A guide arm held in an inactive position has no effect on the operation of the train of gears for that particular cycle.

21. DRUM ASSEMBLY.

a. The drum assembly (fig. 10) consists of the shaft and disks (30), the bars (31), and lugs (32), the step and lock arm (fig. 9), and the gear. Attached to the shaft, and operated by it, are the paper feed cam and the printing cam. Paragraph 23 explains the functions of the paper feed cam and the printing cam. The 27 drum bars are numbered on

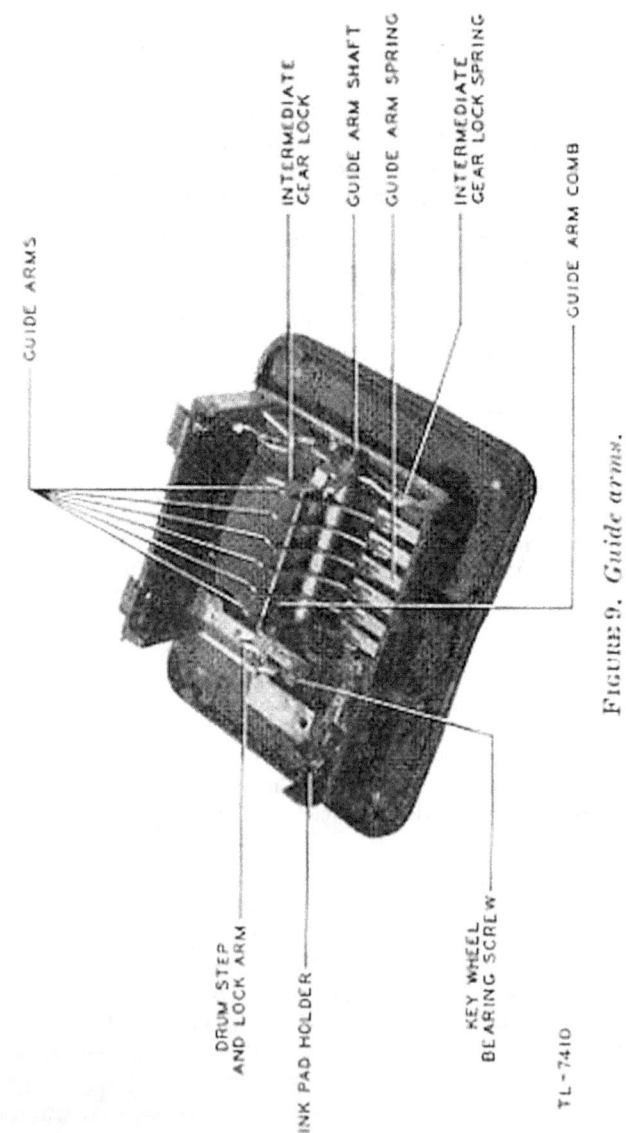

Figure 9. *Guide arms.*

FUNCTIONING OF PARTS — TM 11-380, Par. 21-22

the face of the right-hand drum disk to assist the operator in making the preliminary settings.

b. On each drum bar are two movable lugs. The drum bar lugs may be moved to any one of eight positions. These eight positions are numbered (on a number plate just behind the drum assembly), in the following order: 1 $\overset{0}{\downarrow}$ 2 3 4 5 $\overset{0}{\downarrow}$ 6. The zero positions are noneffective, but the other six are effective positions located directly in front of the six guide arms. The lugs are placed according to the cipher-key list in effect.

c. The drum assembly makes one complete revolution each time the drive knob is rotated, and the effective drum bar lugs are contacted by effective guide arms. The drum bar lugs are forced, one after the other, to the left. In the left position the drum bar lugs act as cogs of a wheel, meshing with the typewheel intermediate gear, which drives the typewheel. The typewheel is turned as many letters as there are bars projecting from the left of the drum. A retractor forces the bars back into neutral position after they have been used. At the end of the operating cycle, a cam on the left-drum disk pushes the drum lock arm into place; simultaneously a projection from the lock arm drops between two cogs of the typewheel gear. The drum remains locked until the typewheel is turned, moving the projection of the lock arm, and releasing the lock arm.

22. **TYPEWHEEL ASSEMBLY AND PRINT ARM ASSEMBLY.**

a. The setting knob (8), indicating disk (7), reproducing disk (6), typewheel (5), and typewheel gear (43), are all mounted on a common shaft and make up the typewheel assembly (fig. 11). A screw in the end of the shaft holds the typewheel assembly in place. The assembly is used to select the letter to be cryptographed or decryptographed and print the enciphered or deciphered letter on a paper tape.

TM 11-380   CONVERTER M-209, M-209-A,
Par. 19   M-209-B (CIPHER)

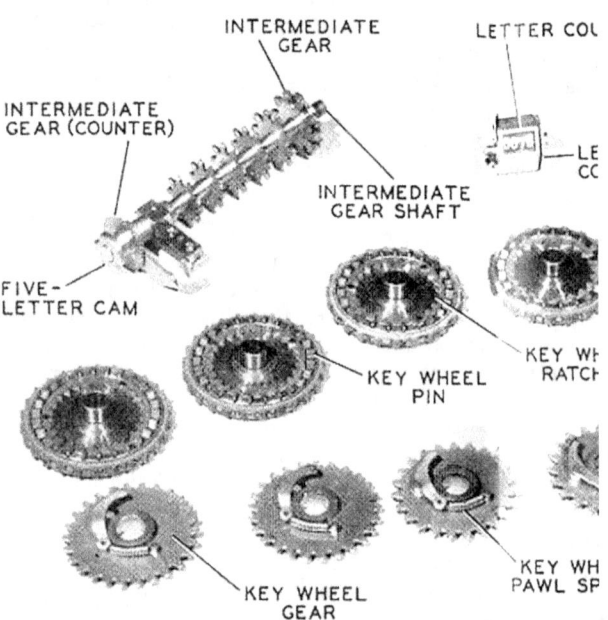

FUNCTIONING OF PARTS   TM 11-380 Par. 19

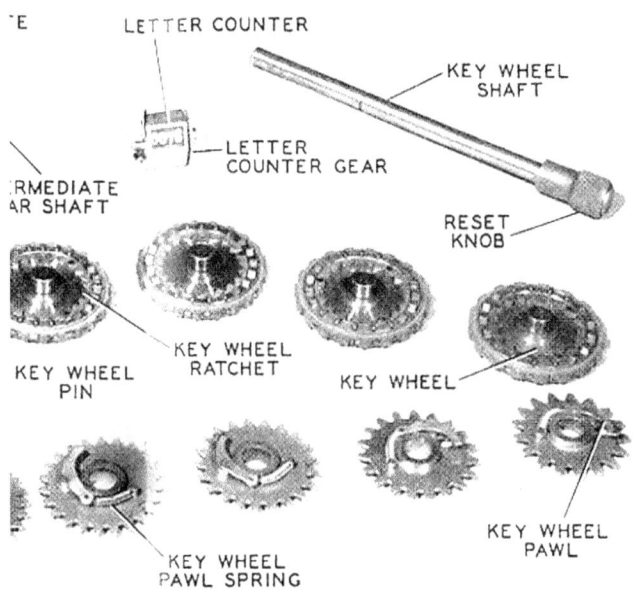

FIGURE 8. *Key wheel assembly.*

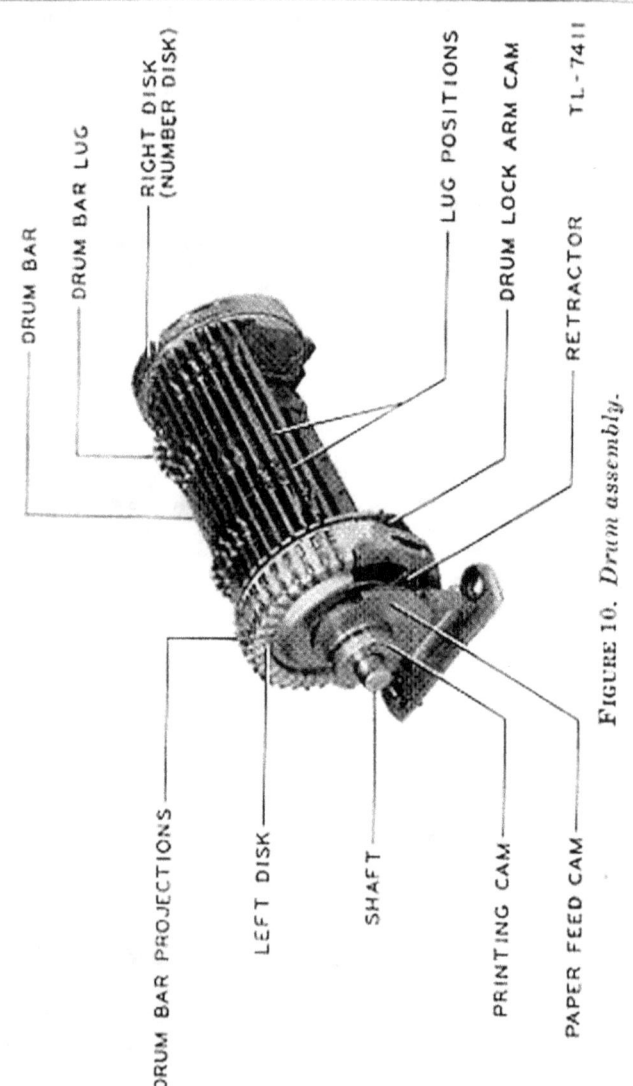

FIGURE 10. *Drum assembly.*

b. The indicating disk, containing the letters of the alphabet in normal order, is set to the desired letter by alignment of that letter with the indicating index mark (3) on the inner lid. During the operating cycle, the intermediate typewheel gear meshes with the effective drum bars and drives the typewheel gear. The typewheel prints the letter in position at the end of the cycle; printing is accomplished through the action of the print hammer. The letter printed may also be seen as the first letter visible on the reproducing disk. If the supply of tape or ink pads should become exhausted, the cipher text may be copied from the reproducing disk, one letter after each operating cycle.

c. The print arm assembly is mounted on the shaft of the encipher-decipher knob and includes the print arm, print hammer, and print arm stop. A spring attached to the print arm and the base of the converter keeps the required tension on the assembly.

d. Printing is accomplished at the end of each operating cycle, when the printing cam (fig. 10) on the drum shaft allows the print arm to be pulled forward suddenly by the print arm spring. The print hammer, a piece of hard rubber clamped in the teeth of the print arm, strikes the tape against the inked typewheel, printing a letter. The printing cam, continuing its cycle, brings the print arm back to its original position.

e. The print arm stop prevents printing of the letter Z when the machine is being used to decipher. A cam on the shaft of the encipher-decipher knob controls the operation of the print arm stop. When the encipher-decipher knob is set in the D position, the printing cam pushes the print arm stop forward and holds it. On the typewheel shaft there is a small pin offset from the letter Z, which rests against the print arm stop when Z is to be printed. As a result, the print hammer is not allowed to strike the typewheel and a blank space ap-

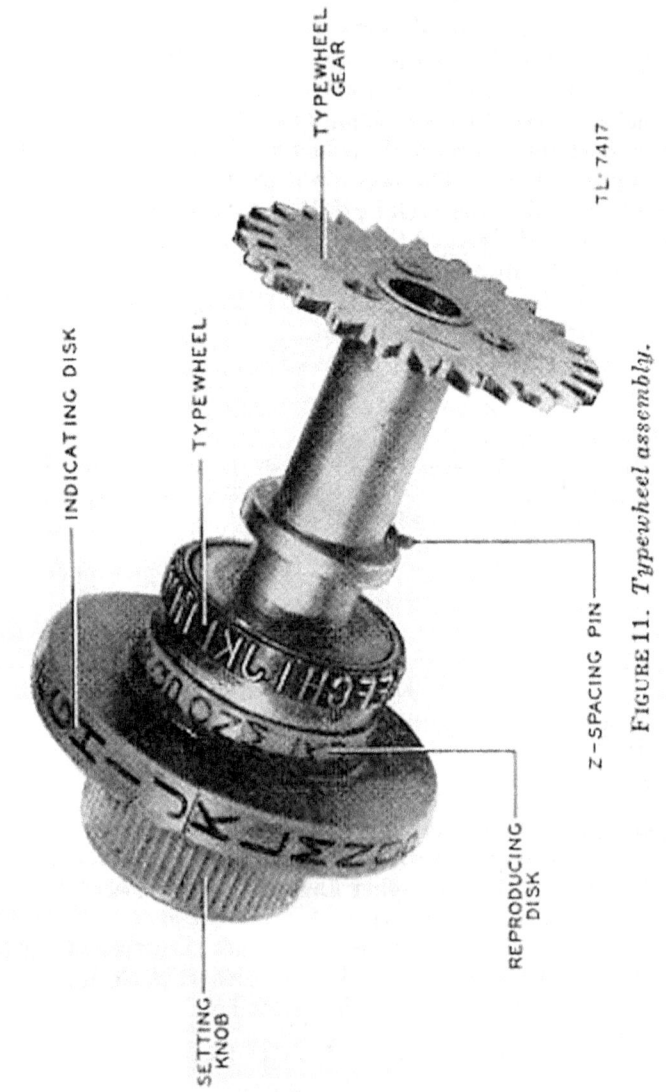

FIGURE 11. *Typewheel assembly.*

FUNCTIONING OF PARTS

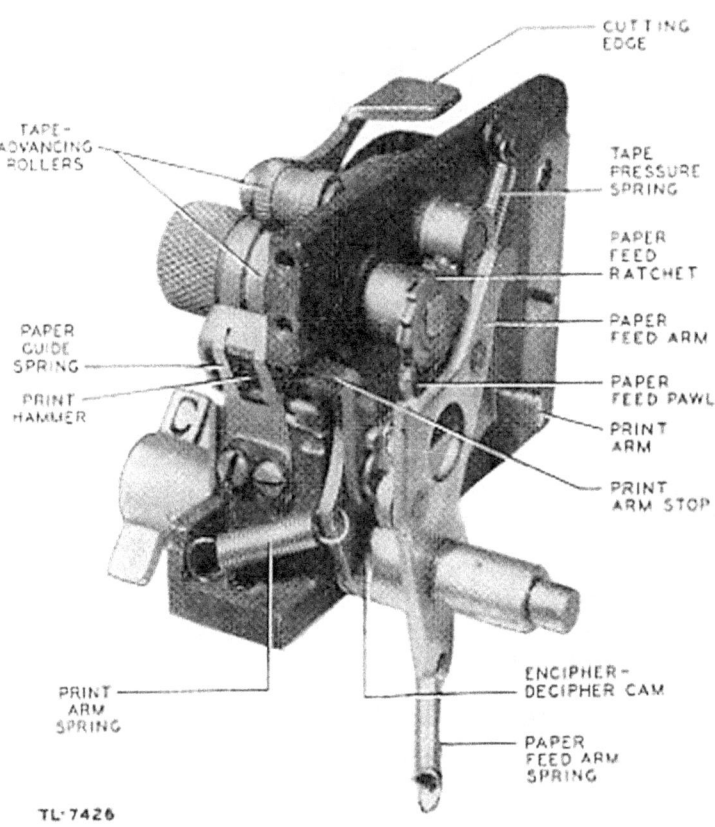

FIGURE 12. *Paper feed assembly.*

pears on the tape. When the encipher-decipher knob is set in the C position, the print arm stop is held back and does not touch the pin.

23. PAPER FEED ASSEMBLY.

a. The paper feed assembly consists of a large cam on the drum shaft (fig. 10), an arm which rides on this cam, a pawl and ratchet, a small 5-letter cam (13), a paper feed stop, and a knob (fig. 12).

b. The revolution of the paper feed cam causes the paper feed arm to move the paper feed pawl and ratchet one notch for each operating cycle, advancing the paper tape one space. Double spacing between groups is accomplished by the 5-letter cam. A projection from the paper feed arm rides on the outer rim of the 5-letter cam which has two indentations on opposite sides. As the projection rides into one of the indentations, the paper feed arm moves the pawl and ratchet two notches, advancing the tape two spaces. After five letters have been enciphered, the projection will again ride into an indentation on the cam and permit double spacing.

c. Automatic spacing is not desired during deciphering, and is prevented by the paper feed stop. The paper feed stop is in contact with the cam of the encipher-decipher knob. When the encipher-decipher knob is set in the D position, the arm of the paper feed stop is raised and aligned on a fixed projection of the drum shaft bracket. The projection of the paper feed arm is prevented from following the contour of the 5-letter cam, resulting in continuous single spacing.

TM 11-380
Par. 24

SECTION IV

MAINTENANCE

24. CARE OF CONVERTER.

a. Preventive Checks. Converter M-209-(*) will offer few maintenance problems if it is operated correctly and cared for properly. In many cases a thorough cleaning and lubrication will remedy mechanical difficulties. As the machine is used from day to day, a few simple checks during operation will help to keep the device in good operating condition. Operators should check the following items:

(1) Spring tension of the various visible springs on machine.

(2) Proper lubrication.

(3) Amount of lateral play in the key wheels on the key wheel shaft (par. 26). (Key wheels must be sufficiently tight to avoid slipping to one side, but not so tight that easy turning is prevented.)

(4) Dried ink on typewheel or dust in operating parts.

(5) Proper positioning of lugs on drum bars.

(6) Tightness of screws on drum base.

b. Cleaning. From time to time certain parts of the machine will require cleaning.

(1) TYPEWHEEL. The typewheel may become caked with ink and print indistinct or illegible characters. Brushing the

typewheel with a small stiff-bristled brush may be sufficient to clean it. If the dried ink has hardened, use a sharp instrument to loosen the ink before applying the brush. Do not damage the letters on the typewheel with the instrument.

(2) GENERAL. When the converter is used in the field, dust may collect in the operating parts and impede their action, especially if the machine has been oiled excessively. If the machine becomes clogged, remove the parts as directed in paragraph 34 and clean with a dry cloth. Lubricate the machine before replacing the parts. Remove the dust from corners and openings occasionally with a small brush. Always close the outer cover when the converter is not in use.

c. Oiling. The oil rod provided with Converter M-209-(*) is attached to the cover of the oil can, and should always be used to oil the machine. The bearings should be lubricated occasionally (for every 256 hours of operation) by placing one to four drops of oil in the lubricating holes provided. The drum bar slots on the left-hand side of the drum should be kept well oiled, but all other moving parts should be lubricated sparingly.

d. Paper Tape Supply. To insert fresh tape into the paper feed mechanism, release the hinged guard which holds the roll of paper in place and allow the guard to tilt forward against the inner lid. Remove the empty spool and place a new roll of tape over the pin. (The tape must unroll in a counter-clockwise direction.) Pass the end of the tape through the slot in the hinged guard, bring the tape forward, and insert it in the tape slot just above the encipher-decipher knob. Push the tape through the tape channel until it appears between the typewheel and the tape-advancing rollers. The tape must pass under the paper guide spring immediately behind the typewheel. Next pass the paper tape between the tape-advancing rollers (fig. 12), while depressing the paper pressure arm.

MAINTENANCE

e. Ink Pads. Additional ink pads will be found in one of the small metal containers held by spring clamps in the outer cover of the machine. To insert a fresh pad, open the inner lid of the converter, use the tweezers to remove the old pad, and insert a new one. The life of the pad, before replacement is necessary, can be prolonged by turning it end for end. The ink pads should be re-inked with the special ink developed for the ink pads, or with any standard purple or black stamp pad ink. Hectograph ink should not be used because it dries the ink pad and makes it unfit for further use.

f. Minor Repair. The operator of Converter M-209-(*) should be able to make certain minor repairs on the machine. Paragraphs 25 through 32 explain the common minor troubles and include information for correcting such troubles. Paragraph 34 explains how to dismantle the machine and limits operator's maintenance to minor repairs.

25. JAMMING.

a. Description and Location. Converter M-209-(*) is jammed when the drive knob will not revolve. Jamming may occur at any phase of an operating cycle and is generally the result of faulty operation. DO NOT USE FORCE IN AN ATTEMPT TO CLEAR THE MACHINE. The operator should first make the following checks to locate the cause of the trouble:

(1) Move indicating disk slightly and realign letter to be enciphered or deciphered. Try drive knob.

(2) Move reset knob until it snaps into place (if not already in place). Try drive knob.

(3) Open inner lid. Rock drum back and forth several times. Try drive knob.

b. Causes. If none of the checks listed clears the jam, the operator must determine whether the trouble is due to one of the following causes:

(1) A DRUM BAR LUG OUT OF LINE, A BENT DRUM BAR LUG, OR A BENT DRUM BAR TOOTH (fig. 10). Open the inner lid. If the drum has been moved through only part of the operating cycle, proceed as follows:

(a) Using the flat side of the screwdriver, push to the right drum bars projecting beyond the left side of the drum. The drum bars must be pushed until flush with left side of the drum.

(b) Turn drive knob until it locks.

(c) Check for a lug not fitted into a hole. Check also for a bent lug, or for a bent drum bar tooth.

(d) If a lug or tooth is bent, straighten it with a pair of pliers and use it until a new lug or bar can be obtained.

(2) BENT GUIDE ARM (fig. 9). Check each guide arm to determine if one is bent and touching a drum bar or the base of a drum bar lug. If a bent guide arm is found, pull it back toward the front of the machine, and turn the drive knob to complete the cycle. Bend the guide arm back to its proper position with a pair of pliers. The guide arm must make contact with the side of the lug projection only. Do not bend the guide arm into the comb (fig. 9), or the guide arm will not operate freely.

(3) EXCESSIVE PLAY IN THE KEY WHEELS. Open the inner lid. Check each key wheel to determine whether one has slipped to the right and become disengaged from the key wheel intermediate gear (fig. 8). Key wheels slip as a result of the loosening of the right-hand shaft screw or of the key wheel bearing screw (fig. 9). Re-engage the key wheel gear, and tighten the right-hand shaft screw and the key wheel bearing screw until the key wheels have no play to the left or right. It may be necessary to tap two or three times on the end of the reset knob before tightening the screws in order to slide the shaft over to its proper location.

MAINTENANCE

CAUTION: When tightening the key wheel bearing screw, do not use too much pressure. The screw is made of very soft metal and is easily broken.

(4) BENT TYPEWHEEL DETENT. The typewheel detent is located below and slightly toward the rear of the typewheel gear. The typewheel detent rides on the typewheel gear and makes the clicking noise heard when the setting knob is turned. If the typewheel detent becomes bent to either side of the typewheel gear, the entire mechanism of the converter may jam. Raise the inner lid and remove the letter counter (par. 34). If the typewheel detent is bent, bend it back to the proper position, and turn the drive knob. See paragraph 35 for information on replacing the letter counter.

26. MINOR KEY WHEEL REPAIRS.

a. Key Wheel Rotates in Both Directions. (1) Move the key wheels to the left or right to determine if there is play on the shaft. If play is discovered, add enough shims under the left-end shaft screw to overcome the looseness, and tighten the screws on both ends of the shaft. Test the rotation of the key wheels.

(2) If a key wheel continues to rotate in both directions after the procedure in the above paragraph has been applied, remove the key wheels according to the directions for dismantling the machine in paragraph 34. Separate the faulty key wheel from its intermediate gear by turning the gear in a clockwise direction, pulling the gear away from the key wheel at the same time. Bend the end of the key wheel pawl away from the intermediate gear, so the key wheel pawl will fit closely against the key wheel when the two are placed together (fig. 8). To fit the key wheel and the intermediate gear together, place the gear against the key wheel, and rotate the gear in a clockwise direction while pushing it against the wheel. Replace the key wheels according to instructions given in paragraph 35.

b. Key Wheels Stick. Key wheels operating sluggishly or sticking in intermediate positions probably are set too tightly on the shaft. Check the key wheel bearing screw to determine whether it has been properly set in the indent on the shaft. If not, slide the shaft until the screw is fitted into the indent. If this is not the trouble, remove enough shims from either end of the shaft to permit free movement of the key wheels.

c. Key Wheel Pins Stick. Place a drop of oil in the key wheel pin slots (fig. 8), and push the pins back and forth several times. If the key wheels are dirty, wash them in a solvent before lubricating the pin slots.

27. MINOR GUIDE ARM REPAIRS. A guide arm may become bent at the point where it runs through the guide arm comb (fig. 9). If a guide arm is bent it may operate sluggishly or may not become effective at the proper time, due to scraping against the side of the comb. Adjust the guide arm by bending with a pair of long-nosed pliers. Be certain not to bend any other part of the guide arm.

28. MINOR DRUM ASSEMBLY REPAIRS.

a. Sprung Drum Bar (*fig. 10*). Remove a sprung drum bar in the following manner: Grasp the left end of the bar just inside the left-hand drum disk, and lift the bar slightly. Now push the bar to the left. When the drum bar has cleared the right drum disk, grasp the right end of the bar and move it in an arc to the left. Work the left end of the bar free of the disk spring. Insert a new bar by following the above instructions in reverse order. It is not worthwhile to attempt to straighten a sprung drum bar.

> NOTE: Drum bars can be replaced by fourth and fifth echelons *only*. This part is not supplied to first, second, and third echelons.

MAINTENANCE

b. Drum Bars Stick. If the drum bars stick, place a drop of oil in each of the drum bar slots on the left-hand drum disk (fig. 10).

c. Drum Not Locking. Bend the projection from the drum lock arm (fig. 9), so that the projection rides on the cam on the left drum disk when an operating cycle is completed. If the trouble is not corrected, the converter must be serviced by a repairman.

29. MINOR TYPEWHEEL ASSEMBLY REPAIRS. If the indicating disk turns hard, check one of the following troubles:

a. Insufficient Space on Key Wheel Shaft. Check the key wheel bearing screw to determine that it is properly fitted into the indent on the shaft. If not, slide the shaft until the screw fits. If there are too many shims, remove as many as necessary.

b. Locking Arm Not Releasing Properly. The projection of the drum lock arm, which locks the typewheel gear, should fit snugly between the cogs of the gear. Adjust the locking arm by bending to the proper position.

c. Bent Typewheel Detent (see par. 25b (4)).

d. Lack of Oil on Shaft (fig. 8).

30. IMPROPER PRINTING.

a. Loose or Missing Print Arm Spring (fig. 12). If the spring is loose, shorten it and use it until another spring is available.

b. Misaligned Hammer Pad. If the rubber pad which is mounted in the print hammer becomes oil-soaked or worn on one side, it will fail to print properly. To remove the pad from the print hammer; remove the typewheel, the paper guide spring, and the hammer guard (fig. 12). Next loosen the clamps on the hammer and lift out the pad. Trim the pad until it is smooth, or turn it end for end, and replace it in the clamps. (Proper size of the print hammer is $\frac{5}{32}$" long, $\frac{1}{32}$" wide, and $\frac{3}{32}$" thick.) Do not clamp the pad too tightly or the outer surface will become rounded.

c. Sprung Paper Guide Spring (*fig. 12*). If sprung, bend the side of the paper guide spring which is out of line, until both sides of the spring apply an equal amount of pressure to the tape. When adjusting the paper guide spring, remember that the print hammer must fall between the two arms of the spring.

d. Sprung Ink-pad Holder. This trouble may result in the printing of only a part of a character. Bend the holder into its proper shape and use it until a new holder can be obtained.

31. **IMPROPER FEEDING OF PAPER TAPE.** The paper tape may feed improperly, or cease to feed, due to one of the following causes:

a. Clogging of the Tape at the Rollers (*fig. 12*). The tape will clog when improperly inserted between the rollers (either placed in crooked or not reaching to the end of the paper pressure arm), or when stuck to the rollers. Remove the clogged tape and insert the end of the tape between the rollers, advancing it to the end of the paper pressure arm. If gummed tape is used and continues to stick, try turning the tape over so that printing appears on the gummed side.

b. Flattened Roller. Regroove the roller with a sharp instrument.

c. Insufficient Lubrication on Top Roller. Oil both ends of the roller.

d. Weak Paper Pressure-arm Spring (*fig. 12*). This spring is located on the inside of the left side-plate, toward the rear

MAINTENANCE

of the machine. Shorten the weak spring to provide sufficient tension, until a new spring is available.

e. Misaligned Paper Pressure Arm. This trouble will cause the paper tape to move out of line and become clogged in the sides of the rollers. Bend the arm until the two rollers are properly fitted.

f. Missing Paper Feed Arm Spring (fig. 12).

32. IMPROPER COUNTING. The letter counter will not operate correctly if improperly mounted. Follow the directions for mounting the counter as given in paragraph 35. The counter will be inaccurate if a tooth is broken off either the counter gear (fig. 8), or the intermediate gear which meshes with the counter gear.

33. COMMON MECHANICAL FAILURES.

a. General. It is impracticable to list all of the failures possible with Converter M-209-(*). A summary of some of the more common mechanical failures is given below as a check list for the repairman, including those which have already been discussed under the operator's "minor repair" headings.

b. Check List for Repairmen.

(1) Defective key wheel feed, allowing key wheels to remain stationary.

(2) Too much play in key wheels on shaft.

(3) Jamming of lock on typewheel gear teeth.

(4) Inoperative drum lock, i. e., drum moves past stop.

(5) Drum out of line due to previous jam cleared by force.

(6) Sprung drum bar.

(7) Bent or burred drum bar tooth.

(8) Bent drum bar lug.

(9) Sticking of drum bar.

(10) Failure in operation of feed stop pawl for key wheels.

(11) Partial advancement of key wheels due to bind in key wheel feed pawl.

(12) Irregular or binding paper feed.

(13) Weaving of paper tape.

(14) Guide arms binding irregularly, or sticking in active or inactive positions.

(15) Weak, detached, or broken spring on paper feed pawl.

(16) Irregular printing due to broken or bent paper guide spring.

(17) Irregular printing due to worn or loose printing hammer rubber.

(18) Failure to print due to weak or broken printer spring.

(19) Broken key-wheel-pawl ratchet spring.

(20) Key wheel pawl slipped out of ratchet.

(21) Key wheel pin sticking.

(22) Failure of typewheel detent (safety catch) to function properly.

(23) Detached or broken typewheel detent spring.

34. PROCEDURE FOR DISMANTLING.

a. Operator. Converter M-209-(*) can be sufficiently dismantled for the operator to make any *minor* repairs necessary by following the numbered steps below:

(1) Remove ink pad.

(2) Remove letter counter (two screws).

(3) Remove key wheel left-end shaft screw.

(4) Loosen key wheel bearing screw (fig. 9).

(5) Withdraw key wheel shaft (fig. 8) by pulling the reset knob (with the screw still in it) to the right, while rocking the key wheels with the palm of the left hand.

MAINTENANCE

(6) Remove typewheel assembly (fig. 11). Pull the ink pad holder back when lifting the assembly out.

(7) Remove key wheels (fig. 8).

b. Repairman. If a converter requires more than minor repair it must be serviced by a repairman. In addition to the dismantling procedure authorized an operator, a repairman will continue dismantling as follows:

(1) Revolve the drum in the usual manner until 27 on the number disk is the only number visible; then remove the drum bar lug number plate (fig. 3, (29)) by taking out the two screws, lockwashers, and spacing washer. (After removing number plate, complete the drum cycle.)

(2) Remove the right side-plate (4 screws). Note the dowel which is fitted into the end of the rear plate of the machine. The side-plate must be pulled straight out in order to prevent bending the dowel.

(3) Remove the intermediate gear assembly (2 screws). Do not bend the dowel between the two screws (fig. 8).

(4) Remove the left side-plate, proceeding as follows:

(a) Unhook the print arm spring and the paper feed arm spring from the spring clip (fig. 12).

(b) Remove the screw on the left of the underside of the base. This screw holds the encipher-decipher knob detent ball and spring in place. Remove the ball and spring.

(c) Remove the screw in the inset on the underside of the base.

(d) Remove the screw on the lower back of the left side-plate.

(e) Remove the screw spring and latch assembly on the upper back of the left side-plate.

(5) Remove the two screws on the bottom of the drum shaft bracket, and lift out the drum. Do not bend the dowel.

(6) Remove the guide arm shaft, guide arms, and intermediate gear lock (fig. 9).

c. Parts Accessible without Dismantling. After the repairman has dismantled the converter as directed in the above paragraphs, a number of parts are accessible without any further dismantling. These parts are as follows:

(1) The paper feed assembly and print arm assembly (parts of the encipher-decipher knob shaft) on the left side-plate (fig. 12).

(2) The paper guide spring and hammer assembly (fig. 12).

(3) Parts mounted on the base casting as follows:

  (a) Ink pad holder and spring (fig. 9).

  (b) Print arm and paper feed spring clip.

  (c) Guide arm spring (fig. 9).

  (d) Intermediate gear lock spring (fig. 9).

  (e) Key wheel feed-arm assembly (fig. 9).

  (f) Intermediate gear release-arm assembly (right side-plate).

  (g) Key wheel feed-pawl spring clip (upper right corner).

35. PROCEDURE FOR REASSEMBLING. To reassemble Converter M-209-(*) follow in reverse order the procedure given above for dismantling. Note the following special instructions:

a. The Guide Arms. Mount the guide arms as follows: Place any guide arm numbered 156 in the first position on the guide arm shaft (counting from left to right). Follow the guide arm numbered 156 with the three guide arms numbered 234. Next, place on the shaft the remaining two guide arms numbered 156, and place the intermediate gear lock (fig. 9) in the extreme right position. The smaller end of the shaft is inserted in the lower bearing in the key wheel bracket, and

MAINTENANCE

the bent ends of the guide arms are placed through the slots in the guide arm comb. Each guide arm must rest on a part of the flat spring. The intermediate gear lock rests on its own spring. The right side-plate must be mounted before any adjustment is made. Then adjust for tension, freedom of movement, and alignment. Adjustments may be made by loosening the three screws holding the guide arm comb in place, and sliding the comb back and forth until the proper alignment is obtained. If necessary, a guide arm which scrapes against the comb may be adjusted by bending it with a pair of long-nosed pliers. Bend only that portion of the guide arm which operates in the slots of the comb.

b. The Left Side-plate. As the left side-plate is slid into position, lift the paper feed arm so it rests on the paper feed cam of the drum. Replace the detent ball and spring in the underside of the base, and hook the springs to the spring clip.

c. Key Wheels. To replace the key wheels, proceed as follows: Insert the key wheel shaft through the hole in the right side-plate so the shaft reaches the position for key wheel number 6. Each key wheel is numbered according to its position with the exception of number 6 which is blank. The key wheel numbers are visible through a hole in the key wheel gear and are engraved on the key wheel pawl. Place key wheel number 6 in position and slide the shaft through it. Follow with each key wheel in reverse order, i. e., 5, 4, 3, 2, 1. Slide the shaft completely through the typewheel assembly. Push the reset knob against the key wheels until they fit closely together in place, and tighten the key wheel bearing screw. (Do not twist off the head of the screw.) Next tighten the two screws at the ends of the shaft and test the typewheel and key wheels to determine if they turn freely, and check for play to right and left. A certain amount of play is permissible for the typewheel, but no play is allowable for the key wheels.

d. Letter Counter. Before mounting, the counter must be set to 0000 or any multiple of five. The 5-letter cam must be properly positioned to assure coordination between the cam and the counter. Proper positioning is accomplished by turning the drive knob a sufficient number of times to bring the dowel pins of the intermediate gear shaft to a vertical position. The counter gear must mesh properly with its intermediate gear, so that a full series of numbers is visible through the letter counter window.

36. INSPECTION CHECK. The following check list should be used after repairs and adjustments have been completed. This inspection check will assure that the machines are returned to service in proper working condition. The troubles listed below are followed by suggestions for correction only where such suggestions are necessary.

a. Encipher-decipher Knob.

(1) Binding of knob. REALIGN LEFT SIDE-PLATE.

(2) No detent in knob.

b. Letter Counter.

(1) Faulty alignment of numbers. MESH TEETH PROPERLY.

(2) Gear out of line.

(3) Poor meshing of gears. ADD OR TAKE OFF SHIMS.

c. Drum.

(1) Drum jamming. CHECK POSITION OF DRUM BAR LUGS.

(2) No detent in bar.

(3) Sprung bar. INSERT NEW BAR.

(4) Sticking bar. CLEAN SLOT OR CHANGE BAR.

(5) Inoperative lock. ADJUST DRUM, AND CHECK LOCK SPRING.

MAINTENANCE TM 11-380
Par. 36

(6) Binding. CHECK ALIGNMENT.

(7) Improperly set bracket slot.

(8) Slipping of drum when intermediate lock is open.

(9) Number disk not pinned.

  d. *Drum Lugs.*

(1) Too loose or too tight.

(2) Improperly fitted in drum bar slots.

  e. *Guide Arms.*

(1) Too weak or too strong. ADJUST GUIDE ARM SPRING.

(2) Too far from, or too close to, pins on key wheel. ADJUST BY BENDING.

(3) Sticking, causing improper encipherment and decipherment. ADJUST BY BENDING.

(4) Improperly adjusted to lugs on drum. ADJUST BY BENDING.

(5) In wrong position, causing false encipherment. CHECK GUIDE ARM NUMBERS; SEE PARAGRAPH 35.

  f. *Intermediate Key Wheel Gears.*

(1) Too much play in key wheel release. USE SHIMS.

(2) Lock arm riding on drum. ADJUST BY BENDING.

(3) Drive gear making contact with drum bar. POSITION DRUM PROPERLY.

(4) Faulty alignment of gears.

(5) Faulty timing of feed arm.

  g. *Paper Feed.*

(1) Defective cam or loose taper pin.

(2) Defective paper.

(3) Jamming.

(4) Weaving of paper. ADJUST PAPER PRESSURE ROLLER.

(5) Inoperative. CHECK FOR FREEDOM OF MOVEMENT.

h. Pins (key wheel).

(1) Sticking. WASH WHEEL IN SOLVENT; LUBRICATE.

(2) No detent. REPLACE KEY WHEEL.

i. Key Wheels.

(1) Defective. REPLACE.

(2) Excessive side play. TIGHTEN RIGHT-END SCREW ON KEY WHEEL SHAFT, OR INSERT SHIM IF NECESSARY.

(3) Incorrectly positioned.

(4) Improper alignment.

(5) Ratchet defective.

(6) Binding and difficult to move.

j. Key Wheel Gears.

(1) Bent. STRAIGHTEN IF POSSIBLE; OTHERWISE REPLACE.

(2) Out of line. REPLACE.

k. Key Wheel Release.

(1) Sticking lever.

(2) Lack of play in reset button.

(3) Excess play in lever.

(4) Inoperative reset button.

l. Printing.

(1) Double print. ALIGN PRINTING HAMMER.

(2) Light on one side; ink pad not centered. ALIGN PRINTING HAMMER.

MAINTENANCE — TM 11-380, Par. 36

(3) Parts of letter not printed. ALIGN PRINTING HAMMER; CHECK TENSION OF PAPER GUIDE SPRING.

(4) Poor spacing.

(5) Prints Z with machine set to decipher. CHECK PIN ON TYPE WHEEL.

(6) Groups irregular. CHECK INTERMEDIATE FEED ARM ON RIGHT OF DRUM.

(7) Letters appearing in groups of 10, 15, or 20, but not 5. CHECK PAPER FEED.

m. Screws.

(1) Loose.
(2) Marred.
(3) Missing.

n. Springs.

(1) Deformed. REPLACE.
(2) Missing.
(3) Unattached.

o. Typewheel.

(1) Binding.
(2) Detent stiff.
(3) Excess play.
(4) Typewheel gear riding on counter shaft.
(5) Inoperative lock. ALIGN DRUM.
(6) Drum lock jamming on typewheel gear tooth.

p. Washers.

(1) Missing.

SECTION V
SUPPLEMENTARY DATA

37. TABLE OF REPLACEABLE PARTS.

NOTE: Order replacement parts by stock number, name and description.

a. Maintenance Parts.

Ref. No. †	Signal Corps stock No.	Name of part and description	Function
..	6E1009 ( )	Converter M-209-(*).	......
34	6E1009A/A2	Arm, guide, #2, #3, #4.	Activates drum bar lugs in positions 2, 3, 4.
34	6E1009A/A3	Arm, guide, #1, #5, #6.	Activates drum bar lugs in positions 1, 5, 6.
..	6E1009A/B1	Ball, encipher-decipher detent.	Holds encipher-decipher knob in position.
31	6E1009A/B5	Bar, drum.	Projects to left during operation and acts as cog of a gear.
..	6E1009A/B15	Bracket, ink pad arm.	Holds ink pad arm.
17	6E1009A/C1	Can, ink pad—with 5 ink pads, cover marked "I", 2⅜" long and ⅞" diameter.	Contains supply of ink pads

SUPPLEMENTARY DATA TM 11-380
Par. 37

19	6E1009A/C2	Can, oil—with dipstick, cover marked "O", 2⅜″ long and ⅞″ diameter.	Contains oil for converter.
Fig. 1 ⑥	6E1009A/C12	Clip, message—steel strip looped over on each end.	Clamps message on front of machine for reading.
Fig. 9	6E1009A/C17	Comb, guide arm—metal, with 6 slots for guide arms.	Controls movement of guide arms.
ʺ	6E1009A/C20	Counter, letter—0000 to 9999, glass enclosed on one side, with one gear.	Counts letters enciphered or deciphered.
ʺ	6E1009A/D2	Dowel, right side-plate—¼″ long.	Aligns right side-plate.
Fig. 10	6E1009A/D10	Drum assembly—complete with disks, shaft, springs, bracket, drum bars, and drum lugs.	Mechanically determines letter to be printed.
ʺ	6E1009A/F5	Foot, rubber base—flat on one side, beveled on top.	Cushions base.
Fig. 8	6E1009A/G1	Gear, key wheel #1—26 teeth.	Controls key wheel No. 1.
Fig. 8	6E1009A/G2	Gear, key wheel #2—25 teeth.	Controls key wheel No. 2.
Fig. 8	6E1009A/G3	Gear, key wheel #3—23 teeth.	Controls key wheel No. 3.
Fig. 8	6E1009A/G4	Gear, key wheel #4—21 teeth.	Controls key wheel No. 4.
Fig. 8	6E1009A/G5	Gear, key wheel #5—19 teeth.	Controls key wheel No. 5.
Fig. 8	6E1009A/G6	Gear, key wheel #6—17 teeth.	Controls key wheel No. 6.
Fig. 12	6E1009A/H3	Hammer, print arm—metal.	Strikes paper tape against typewheel.
ʺ	6E1009( )/1	Maintenance Instructions, and TM 11-380.	Provides information on maintenance and operation.

† Numbers in this column refer to figure 2, page 4, and figure 3, page 7, except where specifically otherwise designated.

63

Ref. No.	Signal Corps stock No.	Name of part and description	Function
42	6E1009A/K4	Key wheel crown #1—26 characters.	Controls guide arm No. 1.
42	6E1009A/K5	Key wheel crown #2—25 characters.	Controls guide arm No. 2.
42	6E1009A/K6	Key wheel crown #3—23 characters.	Controls guide arm No. 3.
42	6E1009A/K1	Key wheel crown #4—21 characters.	Controls guide arm No. 4.
42	6E1009A/K2	Key wheel crown #5—19 characters.	Controls guide arm No. 5.
42	6E1009A/K3	Key wheel crown #6—17 characters.	Controls guide arm No. 6.
..	6E1009A/L1	Latch plate, cover—steel, 1⅝" long, ½" wide, olive drab.	Acts as keeper for cover latch.
Fig. 9	6E1009A/L15	Lock, intermediate gear—metal, with 3 posts extending from center piece.	Locks intermediate gear at end of each cycle.
32	6E1009A/L16	Lug, drum bar.	Fits on drum bar and makes contact with guide arm.
Fig. 1 ⑨	6D2107-210	Message Book M-210.	Form for writing messages.
	6E1009A/P25	Pad, ink—felt roller (saturated with ink, packed in expendable container).	Inks typewheel for printing.
Fig. 8	6E1009A/P1	Pawl, key wheel ratchet #1.	Links key wheel No. 1 to gear No. 1.
Fig. 8	6E1009A/P2	Pawl, key wheel ratchet #2.	Links key wheel No. 2 to gear No. 2.
Fig. 8	6E1009A/P3	Pawl, key wheel ratchet #3.	Links key wheel No. 3 to gear No. 3.

SUPPLEMENTARY DATA

Fig. 8	6E1009A/P4	Pawl, key wheel ratchet #4.	Links key wheel No. 4 to gear No. 4.
Fig. 8	6E1009A/P5	Pawl, key wheel ratchet #5.	Links key wheel No. 5 to gear No. 5.
Fig. 8	6E1009A/P6	Pawl, key wheel ratchet #6.	Links key wheel No. 6 to gear No. 6.
...	6E1009A/R10	Rubber, print arm hammer—approximately 1/2" long, 5/32" wide, 3/32" thick.	Acts as printing hammer.
18	6E1009A/S25	Screwdriver—notched blade, amber handle, 3 7/8" long.	Used to move lugs and pins, and in minor repair of machine.
Fig. 8	6E1009A/S32	Shaft, intermediate gear—4" by 3/16" diameter, complete with 8 gears of various sizes.	Supports intermediate gears.
...	6E1009A/S40	Shim, counter, 0.005".	Used to provide proper meshing of counter gears.
...	6E1009A/S41	Shim, counter, 0.006".	Do.
...	6E1009A/S42	Shim, counter, 0.010".	Do.
...	6E1009A/S67	Spring, drum bar detent.	Holds drum bars in position until they are activated.
...	6E1009A/S50	Spring, cover support—wire, 3/8" diameter, 5 coils.	Holds cover support forward when not in use.
...	6E1009A/S51	Spring, paper feed—wire, 3/32" diameter, 1/4" long, 20 coils.	Returns paper feed pawl to a forward position.
...	6E1009A/S52	Spring, drum, lock arm, friction-aluminum strip, 1" long, rounded at one end.	Prevents floating of the drum lock arm.

† Numbers in this column refer to figure 2, page 4, and figure 3, page 7, except where specifically otherwise designated

Ref. No. †	Signal Corps stock No.	Name of part and description	Function
Fig. 9	6E1009A/S53	Spring, guide arm—aluminum strip, 2⅝″ long, 1¼″ wide.	Presses guide arms forward.
...	6E1009A/S54	Spring, ink pad—aluminum strip, 1¾″ long, ¼″ wide.	Presses ink pad against typewheel.
...	6E1009A/S55	Spring, intermediate gear release arm—wire, $\frac{3}{32}$″ diameter, $\frac{5}{16}$″ long.	Applies tension on intermediate gear release arm.
...	6E1009A/S56	Spring, intermediate gear safety catch—wire, $\frac{3}{32}$″ diameter, $\frac{7}{16}$″ long.	Retains safety catch in normal position.
...	6E1009A/S57	Spring, key wheel feed arm—wire, $\frac{3}{32}$″ diameter, $\frac{9}{16}$″ long.	Retains key wheel feed arm in normal position.
...	6E1009A/S58	Spring, key wheel feed pawl—⅛″ diameter, $\frac{13}{32}$″ long.	Retains key wheel feed pawl in normal position.
Fig. 8	6E1009A/S59	Spring, key wheel pawl—$\frac{3}{32}$″ diameter, ⅜″ long.	Presses key wheel pawl against ratchet.
...	6E1009A/S60	Spring, encipher-decipher detent—$\frac{3}{32}$″ diameter, ⅜″ long.	Presses encipher-decipher detent against encipher-decipher knob.
Fig. 9	6E1009A/S61	Spring, lock, intermediate gear—L-shaped, 1$\frac{5}{32}$″ long.	Presses intermediate gear lock forward.

Fig. 12	6E1009A/S62	Spring, paper feed arm—wire, 3/32" diameter, 1/2" long.	Applies tension to paper feed arm.
Fig. 12	6E1009A/S63	Spring, paper guide—5/8" long, 11/32" wide, aluminum, flat.	Guides paper tape.
Fig. 12	6E1009A/S64	Spring, paper pressure arm—wire 1/8" diameter, 13/32" long.	Holds tape-advancing rollers together.
Fig. 12	6E1009A/S65	Spring, print arm—steel wire, 3/8" diameter, 1/2" long.	Pulls print arm forward to print letter.
..	6E1009A/S66	Spring, print arm stop—steel wire, 3/32" diameter, 3/8" long.	Holds print arm stop in rearward position.
..	6E1009A/S69	Spring, typewheel detent—steel wire, 5/32" diameter, 21/32" long.	Applies tension to typewheel detent.
Fig. 1 (4)	6E1009A/S75	Strap, hand, carrying—brown canvas webbing, complete with swivel eye and snaps, 6 3/4" long, 21/32" wide.	Attaches to side of converter.
14	4A2708	Tape, paper—white, 3/8" wide, ungummed (for Continental U.S.).	......
14	4A2701.2	Tape, paper—white, 3/8" wide, 4" diameter roll, gummed, tropically treated (for overseas use).	......
26	6E1009A/T5	Tweezers 4 1/4" long.	Used in handling ink pads.
Fig. 11	6E1009A/T8	Typewheel-knurled knob, indicating disk, reproducing disk, typewheel, and 26-tooth gear, all assembled in one unit.	Used in selecting and printing letters.

† Numbers in this column refer to figure 2, page 4, and figure 3, page 7, except where specifically otherwise designated.

TM 11–380 CONVERTER M-209, M-209-A,
Par. 37 M-209-B (CIPHER)

b. Screws and Washers.

Ref. No. †	Signal Corps stock No.	Name of part and description	Function
...	6E1009A/S5	Screw, print arm hammer—#3—44 thread, $\frac{5}{17}$" over-all length, threaded part ⅛" long, nickel.	Holds clamp for print arm hammer rubber.
...	6E1009A/S7	Screw, cover support—#32 thread, $\frac{23}{32}$" long, threaded part ¼" long.	Attaches cover support to left side-plate.
...	6E1009A/S8	Screw, encipher-decipher detent—#8-32 thread, $\frac{15}{32}$" long, threaded part $\frac{2}{25}$" long, dull nickel.	Holds encipher-decipher detent and spring in place.
...	6E1009A/S9	Screw, key wheel shaft end—#8-32 thread, $\frac{13}{32}$" long, threaded part $\frac{5}{32}$" long, flathead.	Holds key wheels and typewheel tightly in place.
...	6E1009A/S10	Screws, base rubber foot—#8-32 thread, $\frac{9}{32}$" long, threaded part $\frac{1}{4}$" long, flathead, dull nickel.	Attaches rubber foot to base.
...	6E1009A/S11	Screw, key wheel feed arm bracket—#5-38 thread, $\frac{3}{32}$" long, threaded part ¼" long, nickel.	Attaches key wheel feed arm bracket to base.
Fig. 9	6E1009A/S13	Screw, set, key wheel shaft (key wheel bearing screw)—#8-32 thread, ½" long, threaded part $\frac{11}{32}$" long, nickel.	Prevents slipping of key wheel shaft.

SUPPLEMENTARY DATA

	6E1009A/S14	Screw, paper guide plate—#5-38 thread, ½" long, threaded part ⅜" long, flathead.	Attaches paper guide spring to left side-plate.
	6E1009A/S15	Screw, side-plate—#8-32 thread, ⅜" long, threaded part 5/32" long, flathead, dull nickel.	Attaches side-plate to base.
	6E1009A/S16	Screw, hinge #5-50 thread, 5/32" long, threaded part 3/16" long, nickeled.	Attaches lid hinge or cover hinge to base.
	6L6256-2-1.7	Screw, drum bar number band—#2-56 thread.	Attaches number band to right-hand drum disk.
	6E1009A/W1	Washer, drum lock arm—metal, ½" O.D., 5/32" I.D.	......
	6E1009A/W2	Washer, drum bar lug number plate—metal, 11/32" O.D., 5/32" I.D.	......
	6E1009A/W4	Washer, key wheel, shaft—tin, ¼" O.D., 3/32" I.D.	......
	6E1009A/W3	Washer, lock key wheel bearing—metal, ¼" O.D., 3/32" I.D.	......
	6E1009A/W5	Washer, lock, lid hinge—metal, 3/16" O.D., 5/32" I.D.	......
	6E1009A/W6	Washer, print arm—metal, 7/32" O.D., 11/32" I.D.	......

† Numbers in this column refer to figure 2, page 4, and figure 3, page 7, except where specifically otherwise designated.

TM 11-380
Appendix I

APPENDIX I

PREPARATION OF PIN AND LUG SETTINGS

1. PIN SETTINGS.

a. Prepare a table of the key wheels by listing, in alphabetical order, the letters appearing on the face of each wheel: the first wheel, A to Z; the second wheel A to Z, omitting W; the third wheel A to X, omitting W; the fourth wheel A to U; the fifth wheel A to S; and the sixth wheel A to Q.

b. Prepare a set of 156 lettered cards, 78 of which are marked R (right) and the remainder L (left). Shuffle the cards thoroughly and draw one at a time. Start with A on wheel number 1, and prepare the key list in accordance with the cards drawn: if a card bears an L, cross out the letter; if a card bears an R, do not cross out the letter. Only letters with effective pins are then shown in the key list (table I, page 13). More than six consecutive effective or noneffective pins on any wheel must be rearranged in order to prevent use of such a sequence. A random arrangement, in which from 40 to 60 per cent of the pins are in the effective position is assured by this method.

2. LUG SETTINGS.
To prepare a table of favorable lug settings, proceed with the following steps in the order given:

a. Selection of Numbers. Select a set of six numbers from either group A or group B in appendix II. Sets of numbers selected from group B must not exceed 10 per cent of the total sets selected. The sets are selected at random from the table, and a set is not used a second time as long as other unused sets are available. Sets of numbers from group B should be used at irregular intervals and should not succeed each other in a key list.

b. Rearrangement of Numbers. Rearrange the numbers so that they appear in random order.

c. Distribution of Overlaps. When the two lugs on a bar are both placed in effective positions, an *overlap* results. The total overlap is found by subtracting 27 (the number of bars on the drum) from the total of the six numbers in a set. The overlaps required for each set of numbers have been calculated, and are given with the sets appearing in appendix II. Distribute the overlaps among the numbers according to the following four rules:

(1) Most of the six numbers should be involved.

(2) Overlaps should include numbers which are separated, and numbers which are side by side.

(3) Several small overlaps should be used in preference to one large overlap.

(4) There must not be more than four overlaps between any two numbers. It is permissible, however, for a number to have a combined overlap of more than four. (The number 12 in subpar. *h* below has a combined overlap of five).

The above rules offer a general guide for overlap distribution, but some deviation can be made from all but the rule appearing in subparagraph (4) above, which must always be followed.

d. Checking Placement of Overlaps. The overlaps must be so placed that a single number, or the sum of any two, three, four, five, or all six of the numbers, yields all the values from 1 to 27, inclusive. Remember that the result of two effective

TM 11-380 CONVERTER M-209, M-209-A,
Appendix I M-209-B (CIPHER)

lugs on the same drum bar is one. As an example, in table III there are three effective lugs in column 6, and one effective lug in column 3, giving a total of four. However, two of the effective lugs are on one bar which cancels the effect of one lug, yielding a result of only three. Hence, the proper total for columns 3 and 6 is three (two plus one), and not four.

e. Preparing Lug Setting Work Sheet. The effective lugs (represented by X's) are now entered on a work sheet similar to that shown in table III; lugs in the same column are placed on successive drum bars in as many cases as the overlap condition permits. The completed work sheet should be checked carefully for accuracy with the results of the previous steps. The two zero positions need not be shown on this chart.

f. Preparing Lug Setting Table. Convert the lug positions set up on the work sheet to the form illustrated in table II, page 15, by writing the numbered positions of the lugs opposite the number representing the drum bar. Determine the positions by referring to the number plate (29) at the rear of the drum bar cage.

g. Complete Preparation of Lug Setting. The following example serves to illustrate the preparation of a lug setting. The steps are numbered to correspond to the steps described in subparagraphs 2a to 2d.

(1) Select a set of numbers from group A.

    1, 2, 3, 5, 10, 12 Overlap=6

(2) Rearrange the numbers.

    2, 12, 1, 5, 10, 3

PREPARATION OF PIN AND LUG SETTINGS

(3) Distribute the overlaps.

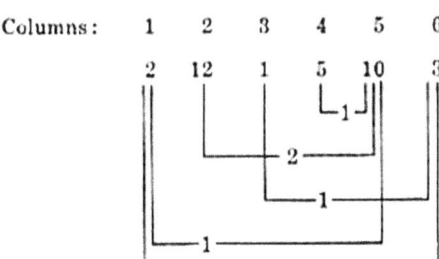

(a) All of the six numbers are involved.

(b) Columns side by side: Columns separated:

      4 and 5   1 and 5
                           1 and 6
                           2 and 5
                           3 and 6

(c) Small overlaps are used in preference to one large one.

(d) Overlaps involving only two numbers do not exceed four.

(4) All values from 1 to 27, inclusive, are obtained. For example:

      1 is given by column 3.
      2 is given by column 1.
      3 is given by column 6.
      4 is given by columns 1 and 6.
      5 is given by column 4.
      6 is given by columns 3 and 4, and so on.

h. Alternate Overlap Distribution. Overlap distribution of the following form produces a good key but does not follow strictly the rules for overlap distribution. Lug settings of this nature should be kept to a minimum in key lists.

```
    1    2    3    4    5    6
    1    5   12   10    3    2
         └₃┘└₂┘        └₁─┘
```

3. PURPOSE. The foregoing limitations are imposed to provide the greatest amount of security possible in the shifting of the alphabets, and to add to the difficulties of enemy cryptanalysts engaged in making a mathematical analysis of the messages.

PREPARATION OF PIN AND LUG SETTINGS

TABLE III. *Position of drum bar lugs work sheet.*

	1	2	3	4	5	6
1.			X			X
2.						X
3.	X					X
4.	X				X	
5.				X	X	
6.				X		
7.				X		
8.				X		
9.				X		
10.		X				
11.		X				
12.		X				
13.		X				
14.		X				
15.		X				
16.		X				
17.		X				
18.		X				
19.		X				
20.		X			X	
21.		X			X	
22.					X	
23.					X	
24.					X	
25.					X	
26.					X	
27.					X	

APPENDIX II
SETS OF NUMBERS AND OVERLAPS FOR LUG SETTINGS

1. GROUP A.

Sets	Overlaps	Sets	Overlaps	Sets	Overlaps
1 2 3 4 8 10	1	1 2 3 5 8 11	3	1 2 4 7 8 9	4
1 2 3 4 7 11	1	1 2 3 5 7 12	3	1 2 3 4 10 12	5
1 2 3 4 6 12	1	1 2 3 5 6 13	3	1 2 3 4 9 13	5
1 2 3 4 5 13	1	1 2 3 6 8 10	3	1 2 3 5 10 11	5
1 2 3 5 8 9	1	1 2 3 6 7 11	3	1 2 3 5 9 12	5
1 2 3 5 7 10	1	1 2 3 7 8 9	3	1 2 3 5 8 13	5
1 2 3 5 6 11	1	1 2 4 5 8 10	3	1 2 3 6 9 11	5
1 2 3 6 7 9	1	1 2 4 5 7 11	3	1 2 3 6 8 12	5
1 2 4 5 7 9	1	1 2 4 5 6 12	3	1 2 3 6 7 13	5
1 2 4 5 6 10	1	1 2 4 6 8 9	3	1 2 3 7 9 10	5
1 2 3 4 9 10	2	1 2 4 6 7 10	3	1 2 3 7 8 11	5
1 2 3 4 8 11	2	1 2 3 4 10 11	4	1 2 4 5 9 11	5
1 2 3 4 7 12	2	1 2 3 4 9 12	4	1 2 4 5 8 12	5
1 2 3 4 6 13	2	1 2 3 4 8 13	4	1 2 4 5 7 13	5
1 2 3 5 8 10	2	1 2 3 5 9 11	4	1 2 4 6 9 10	5
1 2 3 5 7 11	2	1 2 3 5 8 12	4	1 2 4 6 8 11	5
1 2 3 5 6 12	2	1 2 3 5 7 13	4	1 2 4 6 7 12	5
1 2 3 6 8 9	2	1 2 3 6 9 10	4	1 2 4 7 8 10	5
1 2 3 6 7 10	2	1 2 3 6 8 11	4	1 2 3 4 11 12	6
1 2 4 5 8 9	2	1 2 3 6 7 12	4	1 2 3 4 10 13	6
1 2 4 5 7 10	2	1 2 3 7 8 10	4	1 2 3 5 10 12	6
1 2 4 5 6 11	2	1 2 4 5 9 10	4	1 2 3 5 9 13	6
1 2 4 6 7 9	2	1 2 4 5 8 11	4	1 2 3 6 10 11	6
1 2 3 4 9 11	3	1 2 4 5 7 12	4	1 2 3 6 9 12	6
1 2 3 4 8 12	3	1 2 4 5 6 13	4	1 2 3 6 8 13	6
1 2 3 4 7 13	3	1 2 4 6 7 11	4	1 2 3 7 9 11	6
1 2 3 5 9 10	3	1 2 4 6 8 10	4	1 2 3 7 8 12	6

SETS OF NUMBERS AND OVERLAPS FOR LUG SETTINGS

TM 11-380 Appendix II

Sets	Overlaps	Sets	Overlaps	Sets	Overlaps
1 2 4 5 10 11	6	1 2 4 7 9 11	7	1 2 4 6 10 13	9
1 2 4 5 9 12	6	1 2 4 7 8 12	7	1 2 4 6 11 12	9
1 2 4 5 8 13	6	1 2 4 8 9 10	7	1 2 4 7 10 12	9
1 2 4 6 8 12	6	1 2 3 5 11 13	8	1 2 4 7 9 13	9
1 2 4 6 9 11	6	1 2 3 6 11 12	8	1 2 4 8 10 11	9
1 2 4 6 7 13	6	1 2 3 6 10 13	8	1 2 4 8 9 12	9
1 2 4 7 9 10	6	1 2 3 7 10 12	8	1 2 3 6 12 13	10
1 2 4 7 8 11	6	1 2 3 7 9 13	8	1 2 3 7 11 13	10
1 2 3 4 11 13	7	1 2 4 5 11 12	8	1 2 4 5 12 13	10
1 2 3 5 11 12	7	1 2 4 5 10 13	8	1 2 4 6 11 13	10
1 2 3 5 10 13	7	1 2 4 6 9 13	8	1 2 4 7 11 12	10
1 2 3 6 10 12	7	1 2 4 6 10 12	8	1 2 4 7 10 13	10
1 2 3 6 9 13	7	1 2 4 7 10 11	8	1 2 4 8 9 13	10
1 2 3 7 10 11	7	1 2 4 7 9 12	8	1 2 4 8 10 12	10
1 2 3 7 9 12	7	1 2 4 7 8 13	8	1 2 3 7 12 13	11
1 2 3 7 8 13	7	1 2 4 8 9 11	8	1 2 4 6 12 13	11
1 2 4 5 10 12	7	1 2 3 5 12 13	9	1 2 4 7 11 13	11
1 2 4 5 9 13	7	1 2 3 6 11 13	9	1 2 4 8 11 12	11
1 2 4 6 8 13	7	1 2 3 7 11 12	9	1 2 4 8 10 13	11
1 2 4 6 9 12	7	1 2 3 7 10 13	9	1 2 4 7 12 13	12
1 2 4 6 10 11	7	1 2 4 5 11 13	9	1 2 4 8 11 13	12

2. GROUP B.

Sets	Overlaps	Sets	Overlaps	Sets	Overlaps
1 1 2 3 8 13	1	1 1 3 4 6 13	1	1 2 2 4 6 13	1
1 1 2 4 9 11	1	1 1 3 5 8 10	1	1 2 2 5 8 10	1
1 1 2 4 8 12	1	1 1 3 5 7 11	1	1 2 2 5 7 11	1
1 1 2 4 7 13	1	1 1 3 5 6 12	1	1 2 2 5 6 12	1
1 1 2 5 9 10	1	1 1 3 6 8 9	1	1 2 2 6 8 9	1
1 1 2 5 8 11	1	1 1 3 6 7 10	1	1 2 2 6 7 10	1
1 1 2 5 7 12	1	1 2 2 3 9 11	1	1 2 3 3 9 10	1
1 1 2 5 6 13	1	1 2 2 3 8 12	1	1 2 3 3 8 11	1
1 1 3 4 9 10	1	1 2 2 3 7 13	1	1 2 3 3 7 12	1
1 1 3 4 8 11	1	1 2 2 4 8 11	1	1 2 3 4 9 9	1
1 1 3 4 7 12	1	1 2 2 4 7 12	1	1 2 3 5 5 12	1

TM 11-380   CONVERTER M-209, M-209-A,
Appendix II   M-209-B (CIPHER)

Sets	Overlaps	Sets	Overlaps	Sets	Overlaps
1 2 3 6 6 10	1	1 2 4 4 5 13	2	1 2 4 5 5 13	3
1 2 4 4 8 9	1	1 2 4 5 5 12	2	1 2 4 5 9 9	3
1 2 4 5 5 11	1	1 1 2 4 9 13	3	1 2 4 6 6 11	3
1 2 4 6 6 9	1	1 1 2 5 10 11	3	1 2 4 7 7 9	3
1 1 2 4 9 12	2	1 1 2 5 9 12	3	1 1 2 5 10 12	4
1 1 2 4 8 13	2	1 1 2 5 8 13	3	1 1 2 5 9 13	4
1 1 2 5 9 11	2	1 1 3 4 10 11	3	1 1 3 4 10 12	4
1 1 2 5 8 12	2	1 1 3 4 9 12	3	1 1 3 4 9 13	4
1 1 2 5 7 13	2	1 1 3 4 8 13	3	1 1 3 5 10 11	4
1 1 3 4 9 11	2	1 1 3 5 9 11	3	1 1 3 5 9 12	4
1 1 3 4 8 12	2	1 1 3 5 8 12	3	1 1 3 5 8 13	4
1 1 3 4 7 13	2	1 1 3 5 7 13	3	1 1 3 6 9 11	4
1 1 3 5 9 10	2	1 1 3 6 9 10	3	1 1 3 6 8 12	4
1 1 3 5 8 11	2	1 1 3 6 8 11	3	1 1 3 6 7 13	4
1 1 3 5 7 12	2	1 1 3 6 7 12	3	1 2 2 4 9 13	4
1 1 3 5 6 13	2	1 2 2 3 9 13	3	1 2 2 5 10 11	4
1 1 3 6 8 10	2	1 2 2 4 10 11	3	1 2 2 5 9 12	4
1 1 3 6 7 11	2	1 2 2 4 9 12	3	1 2 2 5 8 13	4
1 2 2 3 9 12	2	1 2 2 4 8 13	3	1 2 2 6 9 11	4
1 2 2 3 8 13	2	1 2 2 5 9 11	3	1 2 2 6 7 13	4
1 2 2 4 9 11	2	1 2 2 5 8 12	3	1 2 3 3 10 12	4
1 2 2 4 7 13	2	1 2 2 5 7 13	3	1 2 3 3 9 13	4
1 2 2 5 9 10	2	1 2 2 6 9 10	3	1 2 3 5 10 10	4
1 2 2 5 8 11	2	1 2 2 6 8 11	3	1 2 3 6 6 13	4
1 2 2 5 7 12	2	1 2 2 6 7 12	3	1 2 3 7 7 11	4
1 2 2 5 6 13	2	1 2 3 3 10 11	3	1 2 3 7 9 9	4
1 2 2 6 10 11	2	1 2 3 3 9 12	3	1 2 4 4 9 11	4
1 2 2 6 7 11	2	1 2 3 3 8 13	3	1 2 4 4 7 13	4
1 2 3 3 9 11	2	1 2 3 4 10 10	3	1 2 4 6 9 9	4
1 2 3 3 8 12	2	1 2 3 6 6 12	3	1 2 4 7 7 10	4
1 2 3 3 7 13	2	1 2 3 6 9 9	3	1 1 2 5 10 13	5
1 2 3 5 5 13	2	1 2 3 7 7 10	3	1 1 3 4 10 13	5
1 2 3 5 9 9	2	1 2 4 4 9 10	3	1 1 3 5 10 12	5
1 2 3 6 6 11	2	1 2 4 4 8 11	3	1 1 3 5 9 13	5
1 2 3 7 7 9	2	1 2 4 4 7 12	3	1 1 3 6 10 11	5
1 2 4 4 7 11	2	1 2 4 4 6 13	3	1 1 3 6 9 12	5

SETS OF NUMBERS AND OVERLAPS FOR LUG SETTINGS
Appendix II

Sets	Overlaps	Sets	Overlaps	Sets	Overlaps
1 1 3 6 8 13	5	1 2 2 4 11 13	6	1 2 4 7 7 13	7
1 2 2 4 10 13	5	1 2 2 5 11 12	6	1 2 4 7 10 10	7
1 2 2 5 10 12	5	1 2 2 5 10 13	6	1 2 4 8 8 11	7
1 2 2 5 9 13	5	1 2 2 6 9 13	6	1 1 3 6 11 13	8
1 2 2 6 9 12	5	1 2 3 3 11 13	6	1 2 2 6 11 13	8
1 2 2 6 8 13	5	1 2 3 5 11 11	6	1 2 3 5 12 12	8
1 2 3 3 10 13	5	1 2 3 7 7 13	6	1 2 4 4 11 13	8
1 2 3 4 11 11	5	1 2 3 7 10 10	6	1 2 4 6 11 11	8
1 2 3 6 10 10	5	1 2 4 7 7 12	6	1 1 3 6 12 13	9
1 2 3 7 7 12	5	1 2 4 8 9 9	6	1 2 2 6 12 13	9
1 2 4 4 10 11	5	1 1 3 5 11 13	7	1 2 3 6 12 12	9
1 2 4 4 9 12	5	1 1 3 6 11 12	7	1 2 4 4 12 13	9
1 2 4 4 8 13	5	1 1 3 6 10 13	7	1 2 4 5 12 12	9
1 2 4 6 6 13	5	1 2 2 4 12 13	7	1 2 4 7 11 11	9
1 2 4 7 7 11	5	1 2 2 5 11 13	7	1 2 4 8 8 13	9
1 2 4 7 9 9	5	1 2 2 6 11 12	7	1 2 2 6 13 13	10
1 2 4 8 8 9	5	1 2 2 6 10 13	7	1 2 3 5 13 13	10
1 1 3 5 11 12	6	1 2 3 6 11 11	7	1 2 4 8 11 11	10
1 1 3 5 10 13	6	1 2 4 4 11 12	7	1 2 3 6 13 13	11
1 1 3 6 10 12	6	1 2 4 4 10 13	7	1 2 4 7 12 12	11
1 1 3 6 9 13	6	1 2 4 5 11 11	7	1 2 3 7 13 13	12

©2012 Periscope Film LLC
All Rights Reserved
ISBN #978-1-937684-69-3

www.ingramcontent.com/pod-product-compliance
Lightning Source LLC
LaVergne TN
LVHW051849080426
835512LV00018B/3149